NETWORKING
AHEAD
FOR BUSINESS

The best vehicle to get more customers,
make more friends and create more opportunities
for yourself and others.

by Kathy McAfee

Published by: Kiwi Publishing, Inc
Post Office Box 3852
Woodbridge, CT 06525

info@kiwipublishing.com
www.kiwipublishing.com
203-295-0370

ISBN   978-1-935-768-08-1
First Edition: September, 2010
Second Edition: April, 2011
Printed in the United States
Natural paper, no bleach 30% recycled
Kiwi Publishing, Inc., Woodbridge CT
Book Cover Design by Christian LoGrasso
Cartoons by Joe Kohl

Dedication

To Byron

from blind date to loving husband
you are my favorite networking success story.

To those people whose stories appear in this
book, thank you for teaching me about the
value of networking. You have enriched my life.

net · work · ing

Function: noun
Date: 1967

The exchange of information or services among individuals, groups, or institutions; specifically: the cultivation of productive relationships for employment or business.

Source: Merriam-Webster® On-Line Dictionary

TABLE OF CONTENTS

FOREWORD

Networking Ahead for Business is about managing your life smarter, smoother and more productively! As a marketing expert, Kathy McAfee has integrated the wisdom and knowledge gained from her own networking experiences to capture the unique qualities in distinguishing oneself. The process is to expand the space to shorten the distance to any goal. She illuminates how networking is a powerful tool in becoming the master of one's destiny. Kathy frames the strategy and the tactics in an authentic user-friendly format.

I loved reading *Networking Ahead for Business* as it provided me with insights about "excellence in building relationships" for multilevel purposes. The personal story form kept my attention while the content focused on how building one's own distinction creates opportunities. By the end, it is evident that the clearer we are about our own personal brand, our unique distinction, the more readily we attract networking opportunities to make an inspired contribution in our work as well as in our life.

You will find that *Networking Ahead for Business* is a collection of highly professional, personal, poignant, and profound networking insights organized to create reflections into one's own abilities.

As a business owner and an entrepreneur I found *Networking Ahead for Business* to have brilliantly packaged up the various know-hows that will increase both the earnings and the "fun factor" in my professional life. And with these insights, you too can take your professional and personal life to new and memorable levels of success.

- Juli Ann Reynolds, President & CEO, Tom Peters Company

INTRODUCTION

Born to Drive

Congratulations on acquiring this book! Whatever means you used to get it – perhaps you bought it, received it as a gift from a colleague or friend, or checked it out of your local library – it is now yours to enjoy. It is my hope and sincerest wish that it will hold your attention long enough so that you may glean a few "golden nuggets" and that these insights will help you to create a more positive trajectory for your business life.

This book was born through the spirit of networking. Every story and every idea within these pages are natural byproducts of the networking process. They are derived from people helping people in simple ways that have profound effects. That's networking – the art of building and sustaining mutually beneficial relationships before you need them. And it can have a magical effect on your career, your business and your life. It's like turbocharging your vehicle engine. It gives you more go-power.

My goal in writing this book is to heighten your awareness and increase your motivation toward making networking a key strategy now and for the rest of your life. I want to help you shift into a new gear so that you too can become a motivated networker and acquire the highly prized professional skills of a master connector and the intangible assets of a well-connected person.

Learning from My Experience

As a professional speaker and executive presentation coach, I have spent countless hours advising professionals from all disciplines on how they can become the recognized leaders in their field by mastering the art of high engagement presentations and more effective professional networking. I show them how they can project more of their talent, power and influence when they present themselves and their ideas to others. It starts with realizing that your value is not just in what you know and what you do, but whom you know and who knows you.

Known as America's Marketing Motivator, I'm in the business of pushing people out of their comfort zones and challenging their status quo. I equip and motivate business leaders and entrepreneurs, just like you, to the action that you know deep in your heart and head that you need to take in order to push your mission and success forward.

In my seminars and work with people, I often use a car analogy. Driving is an experience we can all relate to. Your network is like the horsepower of a car. A large network will take you farther and faster than a small network. Your network determines the types of goals you can achieve, and how fast you can attain those goals. With a solid professional network in place, you will have greater mobility and access to more and more opportunities for your business and your career.

Your networking ability is like the skill of the driver. A skilled driver, or networker, is comfortable handling obstacles and barriers, driving faster and longer, and avoiding accidents on the way to the destination.

If you have a less powerful car, this book will show you how to build your network and increase your networking skills and confidence. If you have a powerful car, this book will show you how to get the most out of your existing network.

Let's Take a Drive Together

The book is organized into four sections and filled with real life stories, practical tactics and tools you can use immediately to improve your business networking. At the end of each section, you will find a checklist to review to ensure that you are ready to move on to the next step in our networking journey.

Part I: Ready Your Vehicle – Preparing for Networking Success

Chapters 1 through 5 are devoted to recalibrating your attitude and approach to networking to enable to you to do it more effectively. We will begin by establishing a compelling reason why you should prioritize networking in your daily business life. We will then start to clear out the roadblocks and limiting beliefs and behaviors that are currently getting in your way to successful networking. Putting a marketing hat on, we will undertake strategic targeting by identifying who really matters in your network and how to increase your frequency of touch with those that matter most. Lastly, we will review the fundamentals of professional image and why you should be more conscious of the first and last impressions that you make with your networking contacts.

Part II: Start Driving – Effective Networking Techniques

Chapters 6 through 11 examine how you can use mirroring and matching techniques to more quickly establish rapport with anyone. You will discover new things about your own personal brand and get permission to express your personal brand while you network. You will develop a stronger 30-second elevator pitch, one that allows you to start more conversations that can lead to more potentially beneficial relationships. The mantra "Think relationships, not transactions; Think conversations, not sales pitches" will be become an integral part of your networking drive train. We will program in a more efficient follow-up system that will help you cultivate more relationships more easily. And you'll find out why becoming active in your local chamber of commerce and other networking groups is an essential part of your networking drive strategy.

Part III: Accelerate Your Success – Overcoming Obstacles and Special Situations

Chapters 12 through 18 outline why and how social media and on-line networking can help you expand your sphere of influence faster for business purposes. You will learn how to work through your existing network to get warm introductions to higher-level prospects and new connections. You will open up your mind to new ways in which you could spend quality time with important people in your network in order to take those relationships further. And you will learn how and when to slow down in order to go the distance with key people and how to navigate around the barriers, human or otherwise.

Part IV: Arriving at Your Destination - Taking Your Networking to the Next Level

Chapters 19 through 23 raise your networking game to higher levels, stretching yourself to make more significant connections and to give back to others in more significant ways. You will be nearing the state of unconscious competence, of networking without thinking about it and doing it at higher and higher levels of proficiency. You will be in the graduate level coursework of networking – that is, becoming a master connector – someone who knows many people, who is well connected and one who can help to create more opportunities for others as well as yourself.

A Few Special People to Thank

Attorney Judy Gedge, founder of LLCExpress.com, was a critical cog in the wheel of this book's inception. She was the first person to put the idea of networking as a business topic into my head. She asked me to contribute an article to her Business Line newsletter some years back. I went forward to create a one-page article entitled: "Perfect Your Pitch: The Most Important Thirty Seconds of Your Business Day." This was the genesis of my journey into the study of networking. I have been an enthusiastic student ever since. Thanks, Judy!

Heartfelt thanks to Eitan and Stacey Battat, the co-founders of Kiwi Publishing; without them, this book would still be in my head and not in your hands. They have been both an inspiration and great accountability partners as I learned just how much hard work it actually is to publish a book. No one achieves anything great in isolation. It is with and through people that our goals and dreams can come true. It has been a true pleasure to drive this journey with Eitan and Stacey.

To the talented Christian LoGrasso, my book cover designer and brand architect, who has provided so much value to so many projects since we first worked together at ADVO almost a decade ago. Thank you for your brilliance and continued contributions.

To my neighbor and friend Ted Fleming, whose strategic eye and generous guidance were paramount to creating a flow structure and tighter focus for this book. No doubt, the reader will appreciate your golden touch as much as I do.

To my friend Rahna Barthelmess, whose keen marketing sense and abundance of love, support and encouragement kept me confidently in the driver's seat throughout this project. Rahna – you are most definitely in my Top 50!

To Bryn Tindall, the CEO and founder of Horizon Marketing Group, who connected me to key people in the early days of my business start-up who were instrumental in my future direction. Bryn has continued to remain visible and valuable in my professional network and I am grateful for his unique style of business collaboration.

To my dog, Sofiya, who joined me every day in my office as I wrote this book from start to finish. Her upside-down resting positions and relaxed state brought both comfort and comic relief during the long haul.

To my husband Byron, who believed in me, challenged me, kept me on task and forgave my long hours away from the family and periodic mood swings inherent in an undertaking such as this. You are the best.

Finally, to every single person in my professional network, thank you. I am honored and privileged to know you and to have had the opportunity to help you and to receive your help. As a group, you have taught me so much about networking and business. You make it a joy to participate actively in both.

Pass It On

Ultimately, the value of this book is in the sharing. Whatever you do, don't tuck this book away in your personal library, relegated to a pretty spine graphic among your other books – some read, some not, but all now collecting dust. No. Take this book and pass it on. Share it with other people in your network. We can all get better at this thing called networking and professional relationship-building. The very act of sharing this book is a demonstration that you understand the fundamental concepts contained in it and know how to "walk the talk" of networking. It's all about helping others and asking for help.

So without further delay, please turn the page and let's get on with the business of building your professional network.

> *"The book you don't read won't help."*
> -Jim Rohn, American entrepreneur, author
> and motivational speaker (1930-2009)

PART I

READY YOUR VEHICLE
PREPARING FOR NETWORKING SUCCESS

1. YOU COULD ALWAYS TAKE THE BUS

The WHY Behind Networking

Imagine making your way every day having to take the bus everywhere you go? Most people in the world have this reality. We lucky folks with access to automobiles get to drive ourselves where we want to go, when we need to be there. This independence and mobility is really quite a luxury, one that we often take for granted.

I'd like to propose that your personal and professional network is much like that automobile. It will take you where you want to go, when you need to go there. Without a robust network in place, you will be without wheels, dependent on others or just plain stuck.

What Is Networking, Really?

Networking is essentially about building relationships – one person at a time – actively and systematically cultivating those relationships through time.

Networking is not an event or an activity; it is a strategy for life. Networking is an essential skill for every business and professional person – if not every person – regardless of occupation.

By improving your networking skills and maintaining a robust, healthy professional network of friends, colleagues and acquaintances, you will be able to manage your career better, influence more positive change in the world and build business and professional success for yourself and others.

To do this successfully, I suggest that you follow the advice of Diane Darling, author of *The Networking Survival Guide: Get the Success You Want by Tapping into the People You Know*. She says, "Networking is the art of building and sustaining mutually beneficial relationships." I'd like to add "before you need them" so that they are in place when you need them. That's the value of networking.

But wait a minute.

Why Network? You Already Have a Job

Networking is most commonly associated with job-seeking. It's what you do when you've been laid off, downsized or fired and need to find gainful new employment fast. It's a dreaded activity for most people, especially when they haven't stayed in touch with people they've worked with in the past, and now it's time to make those awkward phone calls. They go something like this:

> Hello, John. This is Kathy. Do you remember me? We used to work together at XYZ company. Sorry that I haven't been in touch lately. Sorry that I didn't return your phone calls when you got laid off. It's just that I was really busy on that project. Anyway, I've just been laid off and I need your help.

The calls may not go exactly like this, but they are uncomfortable and very hard to make. They are also interesting to receive. But you've got to make those calls. Your livelihood is at stake.

Now imagine what that call would sound like, feel like and be like if you had stayed in regular touch with your past colleagues? Perhaps they would even call you once they heard the news. Would they be more willing to offer you assistance and support? Chances are, yes they would.

Networking for Career Management

Networking is a critical component of good career management. It is something that you do throughout your work life, when you are working and when you are not. If it helps you to do it, think of it as "network or not work." By having a robust professional network, you will be able to weave and bob and change jobs, career paths and start entrepreneurial ventures more easily. Your supporters will be behind you. They will be connected with you. They will know what your dreams and goals are. They will help you solve your career challenges, if you practice ongoing networking and good relationship management skills.

Why Network? You Already Know Everyone

Some of you may feel that you have plenty of friends, and your need to add more is not that pressing. Who has the time to make new friends and maintain new friendships? My life is full as it is!

Part of what makes life rich and full is the presence of strong relationships, true friendships and strong connections. Money comes and goes, jobs come and go, and yes, some relationships come and go too. Your ability to develop a pipeline of good connections will help you maintain your happiness, your wealth, opportunities and positive influence in the world.

Networking for Greater Personal Influence

Think about networking from a personal influence point of view. Imagine what good you could do in the world if you have more supportive people on your side. What are you passionate about, and what changes do you want to see in your community, your country, your world? What non-profit organizations are you committed to helping? What causes and social or environmental problems ignite your fire? By sharing these personal passions and convictions with others in your personal and professional network, you can effect more change.

Here's a story of how it worked for me recently. I met a woman entrepreneur for networking coffee. She was a health coach who was trying to figure out how to go to market with her brand and unique services and philosophy. In the course of our networking discussion, I shared some personal information that I was a foster-care parent and was hoping to adopt the two boys living with us. She immediately latched on to this and began to ask me many questions. She and her family had been thinking of adopting a child but didn't know where to go or how to begin the process. As a result of our conversation, she and her husband signed up for a foster-care orientation class and within one year had a 2-year-old girl living in their family. Imagine how I felt when I received the adoption announcement card from her family? Networking had once again produced magic in the world and had changed the lives of other people for good. That's what I call personal influence.

Why Network? You're Not in Sales or Marketing

Some people think that networking only serves those folks who are responsible for business development or sales and marketing. If your specialty lies in a different area, why would you be concerned about networking if you are not responsible for generating new business opportunities?

The answer is because you can. You can have an impact on the business by leveraging the people you know. You can help your organization solve problems better, faster, cheaper by accessing the expertise of the people in your professional network. You may even be the unexpected one who introduces your organization to a major growth opportunity by connecting the new people with new ideas. You potentially have the special power if you learn to harness your professional network.

I was invited to speak at a networking group focused on technology startups. I was speaking alongside a woman named Merrie of SBIR, Small Business Innovation Research, a government-funded program that I had not heard of before this. I took the opportunity to call Merrie before the event and introduce myself. We got to know each other over the telephone, and when we arrived at the night of the event, rapport was already established.

After that event, Merrie and I stayed in touch. She introduced me to the world of high technology startups and showed me how her team at SBIR was match-making inventors and innovators with large companies in order to commercialize and bring to market great ideas that could change the way we solve problems in the environment, health care, national defense/security and more. This was a whole new world to me and one that I hadn't considered serving until I met Merrie.

Merrie and her boss Deb have hired me to speak three times at their regional and national SBIR conferences. I have met hundreds of brilliant innovators who want to take their great ideas and create commercial success. As it turns out, these people also need to improve their networking and presentation skills. My half-day workshops "Perfect Your Pitch" have been very popular at the conference and have changed the way many of these technical professionals communicate and present their ideas during and after the conference.

This story illustrates how business opportunities can be created not only for you, but for others, as the new connections, new ideas and new inspiration cascade across many spheres of influence. Imagine what business opportunities you might spur on by improving your networking skills and confidence.

"Now here comes the big ones. Relationships! We all got 'em; all want 'em. What do we do with 'em?"
-Jimmy Buffet in his song *Fruitcakes*

2. CLEAR THE ROADBLOCKS

Things that Get in Your Way

ROADBLOCK NO. 1:
SOCIAL RELUCTANCE

Networking for Introverts, Shy Guys and Gals

Networking does not come naturally for most people. In fact, it can be quite terrifying to walk into a room full of people you don't know. There can be moments of reluctance even for the most outgoing extravert. Fears, hesitations, doubt and awkwardness well up inside of us to such heightened levels that it becomes a significant emotional event. We don't like it, so as a defensive measure, we avoid it. I call this social reluctance.

This is especially challenging for people who identify themselves as introverts by nature or those who are shy. You may already know that shyness and introversion are not the same thing. Introversion is a personality trait that usually lasts a lifetime. Shyness, on the other hand, is an emotional state that can be overcome.

Carol Bainbridge, who writes about shyness and introversion, suggests that while an introvert may also be shy, introversion itself is not shyness. Basically, an introvert is a person who is energized by being alone or with one or two people at most. Being in crowds of people (i.e., parties, conventions, networking meetings) literally exhausts that person. Have you ever felt that way?

Are You an Introvert?

Ms. Bainbridge explains that "Introverts are more concerned with the inner world of the mind. They enjoy thinking, exploring their thoughts and feelings. They often avoid social situations because being around people drains their energy. This is true even if they have good social skills. After being with people for any length of time, such as at a party, they need time alone to recharge."

If this description fits you, you may be an introvert, and that's perfectly fine. Networking and relationship-building is not the exclusive dominion of extroverts. You too can be successful with people, relationships and yes, networking. You will do so in a way that works best for you. Just keep reading.

Are You Shy?

When I was in college, I had the privilege of sitting in the classroom with the brilliant and charismatic professor, Philip Zimbardo, Ph.D., of Stanford University. His psychology classes were "standing room only." Shy or not, many of us attended his lectures because the topic, quite frankly, was vitally important to our futures (not to mention our weekends).

In his groundbreaking book "Shyness: What it is, What to do about it" Dr. Zimbardo reveals that shyness is pervasive, with as many as 40 percent of people in his research study considering themselves shy. If you're shy, you are not alone. There are millions of shy people all around us.

Shy on the Outside - Torn Up on the Inside

Dr. Zimbardo's study presented a surprising portrait of those with the shy condition. Their mild-mannered exterior conceals roiling turmoil inside. The shy disclosed that they are excessively self-conscious; constantly sizing themselves up negatively and overwhelmingly preoccupied with what others think of them. While everyone else is meeting and greeting, they are developing plans to manage their public impression (if I stand at the far end of the room and pretend to be examining the painting on the wall, I'll look like I'm interested in art and won't have to talk to anybody). They are consumed by the misery of the social setting (I'm having a horrible time at this party because I don't know what to say and everyone seems to be staring at me). All the while their hearts are pounding, their pulses are speeding, and butterflies are swarming in their stomach – physiological symptoms of genuine distress.

Being shy can be extremely uncomfortable, if not emotionally painful. Check out Dr. Zimbardo's web site www.shyness.com for tons of up to date information, surveys to complete, scales and more to help shy folks overcome their social reluctance with confidence.

An Unusual Case of Narcissism

Mark Shepard, master practitioner and trainer of Neuro Linguistic Programming (NLP), the study of how you run your brain, believes that shyness is a form of narcissism, a trait where a person is overly concerned with self-image and ego. Shepard, a recovered "shy guy" himself, works with shy people to help them clear their limiting beliefs and negative emotions. His program "Clear the Fear" helps shy people and others learn how to get out of themselves and get comfortable conversing and connecting with other people. He even wrote a song about it. It's hysterical. Here are a few lyrics from Mark Shepard's song "Narcissism":

Narcissism, narcissism
you know you're really living
When you're looking through the prism of
good ole narcissism

if you want to get ahead in life
you better get this right
people don't want to hear about you
They want you to hear about them!

Narcissism, narcissism
you know you're really living
When you're looking through the prism of
good ole narcissism

What I've thought about you is all wrong
It's been all about me all along
And what I think about you is all about me
So we might as well sing this song...Together!

Shared with permission. © 1998-2010 by Mark Shepard All Rights Reserved.

For more inspiring and entertaining songs, go to www.MarkShepardSongs.com

The good news is that shyness can be overcome. In fact, practicing networking and learning the skills of conversation can be an excellent way to get rid of the shyness problem. Like any learned skill, it will be uncomfortable at first, but after time, you will get good at it. With networking, you also experience an extra benefit: You make new friends and get more opportunity. Why stay trapped inside your narcissistic shy self, when you can come out and play with the rest of us? Once free of your shyness, you will never look back.

How Can You Do it More Comfortably?

My advice to introverted and shy people is to keep in mind that networking is nothing more than building relationships one person at a time. Your energy and focus should be on one person at a time. Find ways and venues that allow you to maintain your personal energy and interest. This book will give you new ideas on just how you can do that.

"The way you overcome shyness is to become so wrapped up in something that you forget to be afraid"
-Claudia "Lady Bird" Johnson, wife of
Lyndon B. Johnson (1912 - 2007)

ROADBLOCK NO. 2:
COMFORT ZONED

Hanging Out with People You Already Know

To be an effective networker, you must continually meet new people and add them to your professional network. Just hanging out with the people you already know is not going to grow your sphere of influence. Imagine if you had adopted this limiting attitude when you were in elementary school? You'd only know the people in your sixth grade class. Not good.

Life has a way of pushing us out of our comfort zones. We move to new places, attend new schools, work for different companies, drive on new roads. In fact, it's really hard not to meet new people throughout your life. So unless you are in the witness protection program, go ahead, put yourself out there, extend your hand and meet new people. It's good for you.

But for some reason, meeting new people in the context of networking takes on a whole new level of hesitation. It can create the same physiological response as public speaking (and we know how some of you feel about doing that). Ultimately, it's fear and uncertainty that stops you.

This reminds me of a personal story when I experienced extreme levels of hesitation that resulted in hermit-like behavior. When I was in sixth grade, my family moved to a new community, which meant a new school for me. It was toward the end of the school year, but still it was traumatizing for a young girl whose whole life was built around her friends, her school and her neighborhood. I was somebody there. Now, I would have to start all over again. It was exhausting just thinking of it.

So I stayed in my room for a full three months after moving to the new house. I didn't go outside and play with new kids. I went to my room immediately after school every day. During the summer, I stayed inside where it was safe. I practically missed the entire summer. I was pissed off, sad, scared, lonely and becoming a bit depressed. The babysitter didn't notice.

Then the new school year started, and I was forced to come out of my shell. It was a new year, new school (junior high school now) for everyone. We were all in the same boat. Everyone had to make new friends. I was forced out of my comfort zone. My self-induced, extended pity party was officially over. Thank goodness, as I could now get on with the business of living and learning.

So what do you have in common with a 12-year-old girl who was traumatized by a changed environment? You're not 12; you may not even be a girl, but no doubt you too have experienced something like this in your life. It's an imaginary roadblock that becomes quite real and powerful and can be personally and professionally disabling.

So the next time you find yourself declining to attend a conference or networking meeting, ask yourself: "What am I afraid of?" "What's the worst thing that could happen to me?" Or better yet, ask yourself, "What's the best thing that could happen to me?"

It's time to come outside and play, make new friends and create new opportunities. President Franklin Roosevelt said, "There is nothing to fear but fear itself." He had a point.

"Don't be afraid to expand yourself, to step out of your comfort zone. That's where the joy and the adventure lie."
-Herbie Hancock, American pianist, bandleader and composer.

ROADBLOCK NO. 3:
LAZY AND UNDISCIPLINED

The Shortest Path to Mediocrity

I'm going to hit you hard here. Networking takes effort. It takes personal discipline. It takes commitment and follow-through. Most of us are just too lazy, undisciplined or disorganized to do it well. We start, and then we stop. We do it for a while, and then we quit. If something bad happens (e.g., get laid off from the job), we quickly start networking again. It's as if networking is behind a glass case that reads, "In case of emergency, break open."

Networking for the Health of It

Networking is like exercise and eating right. It is a no-brainer for short-term and long-term health. Exercise regularly, eat nutritious foods, sleep well, limit the toxins and you may just keep yourself out of the hospital. You'll look better and feel better. You'll potentially live longer and live better.

With effort, it will become your new lifestyle, an automatic daily routine. You'll wonder how you ever lived without doing it. But most of us would rather take a pill, go through surgery or just live a fat, high-risk life than put exercise and healthy living into our daily routines. Crazy, isn't it?

Protecting Your Greatest Assets

"Anything worth having is worth working for," some wise person once said. Yes, your health is worth it. It is your greatest asset. Without your health, you will be severely limited. It's a game changer. Ask anyone who's run the cancer gauntlet.

After your health, your next greatest asset, I propose, is your relationships. Think about the special people in your life who make living rich and meaningful for you. What are you doing to protect this asset? Investing time and effort in those relationships?

Or ignoring them and taking them for granted? Be honest now.

Relationships are at the very heart of networking. They are the big prize in networking. Long-term, mutually beneficial relationships are what you are working toward. Therefore, it only makes sense that some effort will be required to create them and to maintain them. When it comes to relationships, lazy doesn't last long. Couch potatoes don't make good husbands (or wives for that matter), nor do they make good friends or good contacts.

What's so cool about this roadblock is that it is 100 percent in your control. You can do something about it. You don't need external solutions to put it into play. Just add effort and sustain it over a period of time until it becomes a personal habit. Discipline yourself, and make networking and relationship-building a daily priority in your life. If you do this, you'll feel better. More people will care about you. You will care about more people. This is good.

"You can't teach people to be lazy - either they have it, or they don't."
-Dagwood Bumstead, the main character in
the long-running comic strip Blondie

ROADBLOCK No. 4:
SHORTAGE OF TIME

How Are You Using Your 86,400 Seconds Per Day?

"There's not enough time in the day." Don't you love this excuse? It is indisputable. Everyone has the same problem. The busier we get, the more important we feel. How cool is that?

This is not so cool if it keeps you from doing what's important in your life. Never forget that your *To Do* list is not the same as your priorities. Not all tasks are equally important. We have choices. Not just excuses.

Let me share a story that changed how I view time. It was shared to me by the head of my martial arts academy, Grand Master Yu, who is a Judo Olympian, an eighth-degree black belt in Tae Kwon Do, Judo and Hapkido and is on the council the World Korean Judo Society. Clearly, he is an influential man in the global community of martial arts and has positively impacted many lives in his 30-plus years of running martial arts schools, including mine.

One day, when I was feeling particularly overwhelmed (and apparently showing it to others with my body language and energy), he took me aside and told me a story in his broken English and with his charming Korean accent that I have grown to love during my studies with him. He said:

> Let say, I give you 'tousand' dollars every day. You spend as you wish. What you not spend, you give back to me. Next day, I give you another 'tousand' dollars. You spend. What you not spend, you return to me. Next day, same thing. [pause] Tell me, how you spend the money?

> [pause]

Now, instead of 'tousand dollars, I give you 24 hour. I give you 24 hour each day. You spend it as you like. What you don't spend, I take back at end of day. Next day, I give you another 24 hour. Next day, you get another 24 hour. [pause] Question: how you spend your time?

I was dumbfounded, speechless and utterly transformed with this story. I realized that I get this precious, valuable and seemingly unending gift of time. A fresh supply of time – 24 hours every day! That's 1,440 minutes each day or 86,400 seconds each day. Wow! If that were money, I'd be rich!

But unlike money, you can't save time. You can't accumulate it and get compounding interest on it. You can't put it in a bank account, invest it in the market and hope that it grows. Time comes as quickly as it goes. When it's gone, it's gone. But you do get a lot of it, and you have choices as to how you use it.

I tell you this personal story so that you too may adopt a new attitude about time. This is your opportunity to stop making excuses about time and start embracing it as a gift.

While there will always be pressures and demands on your time, ultimately it is yours. You choose how you spend it. Why not spend a little of it each day in building and maintaining relationships? That, my friend, will pay you rewarding dividends.

"We realize our dilemma goes deeper than shortage of time; it is basically a problem of priorities. We confess, we have left undone those things that ought to have done; and we have done those things which we ought not to have done."
-Charles-Camille Saint-Saëns, French composer (1835–1921)

ROADBLOCK No. 5:
TECHNO-PHOBIC VERSUS TECHNO-ADDICT

Misusing Technology to Your Determent

Is technology your friend or foe when it comes to networking and relationship-building? Imagine living without your cell phone, BlackBerry® or iPhone®. Was there life before Facebook®, LinkedIn® or Twitter™? Of course there was. More advances in technology will be introduced after this book is published and will continue to be introduced on a daily basis.

How Do You Keep Up with All of It?

The good news is that we human beings are learning machines. Even as we age, our brains continue to make new neurological connections, our bodies regenerate and we can learn new skills and tasks. But for some of us, the learning process involves a fair amount of complaining.

Technology-Life Balance

In order to strike a healthy balance in using technology to enhance your relationships, you need to keep a few things in mind:

- **Technology is not going away.** It continues to evolve, and you must evolve with it. If you bury your head in the sand and decide that you are not going to participate in social media, for example, you will become outdated quickly. Your skills, knowledge and experience will also become dated.

- **Technology is your servant, not your master.** Like any tool, technology is only as good as your ability to use it, understand it and control it. "The right tool for the right job," my husband reminds me when we are tackling home/garden remodeling projects. When networking and relationship-building, please remember that technology creates new communication channels, additional ways of staying in touch with the people that you care about. But don't become a slave to it. Don't let technology alter the fundamental ways in which you relate to other people.

- **Technology only temporarily hides your flaws.** The song "I'm So Much Cooler Online" from country singer Brad Paisley reminds us of how easy it is to appear to be something you are not when you present yourself on social media sites. Because networking is fundamentally about relationships, you must reveal the real you. Online and offline, you must bring the real you to the table. Anything else would be phony, exhausting and ultimately unsustainable.

"Yes, I love technology, but not as much as you, you see.
But I still love technology. Always and forever."
-Kip's wedding song from the movie *Napoleon Dynamite*

---

3. WHAT ROAD TO TAKE?

Who Really Matters in Your Network

So many roads, so little time. When it comes to networking, everybody is a potential new connection for you. You never know who could bring value into your life. It's mind-boggling to think of all the time you could spend meeting new people and developing these new relationships. And while I believe that everyone does have value, I believe we must strive to be more targeted in our approach to networking.

The reality is that you have a limited amount of time and energy. Since networking is not your full-time job, it's time to figure out who is most important to you and with whom you will invest more of your time, energy and talent in developing a lasting relationship.

Who Is in Your World?

No doubt you know many people from different areas of your life. You work with some, you play with some and you serve on committees with some. The question is: How many people do you know who know you? The average that most people have is around 250. Perhaps you have a few less; perhaps you know a few more. It's a good exercise to make a list of all the people you have met who know you.

My World Exercise™

Think of the people you have met and who know you. List them by the different groups that you associate them with:

- family
- friends
- neighborhood
- work colleagues

- clients
- past job associates
- exercise/fitness groups church or spiritual communities
- community service or volunteer groups
- hobbies
- college friends
- school/kids/scouts/sports

You can download a free template of the My World Exercise™ worksheet at NetworkingAhead.com

I recommend that you do this exercise at first without access to your computer database or cell phone. You will probably be able to generate a list of several hundred people. Once you have that list, then access your address lists loaded on your cell phone, computer and social media sites and look over the holiday cards that you've sent and received in the past. Watch how the list of people that you know grows. How many people are on your list now? Are you surprised? This is a glimpse at who is in your current network. Keep this list handy.

Who Is in Your Inner Circle?

What do all these people have in common? You. You are the connecting thread, the link to all these people. They are in your life and in your sphere of influence.

Now, I'd like you to think in pictures. Imagine a ring of concentric circles, like the logo for the Target® store or a bull's-eye target for an archer. Seen from a networking point of view, the common center point is you. Yes, you are the center of the universe!

Surrounding you and your center point is a small group of people who matter most to you. They love you and care for you and would do anything for you. Who could you share your biggest dreams, fears, concerns and triumphs with? Who would give you candid, critical feedback, even when you didn't ask for it? Who comes to mind when you read this description? Perhaps members of your family or your best friends? Write their names down.

Now think a little more broadly about the people closest to you in your career/work life. With whom do you have a good relationship? Who would call you back promptly if you left a voice mail? Who would go out of the way to help you out if you asked? Whom do you respect, admire and care about? Write their names down.

Your Top 50 Contacts

What you have begun to build is the list of your Top 50 contacts – the 50 most important people to you in your network. I support the idea that our personal and professional networks cross over. In fact, my mother, father, husband, uncle and sisters-in-law have helped me to achieve my professional goals many times over. Why would I exclude them? They care the most for me of anyone I know.

In making my list of my Top 50 networking contacts, I have five basic criteria that I like to meet. You may have more qualifying factors, but here are some simple guidelines you might consider:

1.   You have a good relationship with this person.
2.   You care about this individual as a person.
3.   This individual cares about you as a person.
4.   You can help this person achieve his or her goals.
5.   This person can help you achieve your goals.

Now, with these criteria in mind, who comes to mind as members of your Top 50 networking contacts? Note: you can write them down in any order. Hierarchy is not important.

So what do you do with your Top 50 contact list when you create it? You make these relationships a priority by putting more time and attention into them. I recommend you practice a higher frequency of touch with these important people. Check out this strategy:

50-5-10-2 Strategy

This strategy was shared with me by Angelo Rossetti, an avid networking and tennis professional. On August 9-10, 2008,

Angelo and his identical twin brother, Ettore, broke the world record for the longest tennis rally, successfully completing 25,944 consecutive strokes during a period of 14 hours and 31 minutes. (Now that's bladder control!)

Angelo taught me a great deal about effective networking when I first launched my own company in 2005. One of the ideas that stuck with me was the idea of knowing who my Top 50 contacts are and practicing the 50-5-10-2 strategy.

Here's how it works:

- 50: Identify your Top 50 contacts.

- 5: Reach out and touch base with them once every five weeks or so.

- 10: That means you will be reaching out to 10 people per week.

- 2: That equals two people per day (Monday to Friday; you can take the weekend off!).

Can you do that? Touch base with two people each day? And not just any two people – two people who are among the most important to you in your professional network. If you commute, consider reaching out to one person during your morning com-mute and one person on your afternoon commute. This assumes you can speak on the phone safely while you drive.

Find out what communication channels your Top 50 folks prefer. Are they telephone people? E-mail people? Texting people? Do they like to sit down with you for coffee or lunch? Are they golfing people? Quality of communication counts when you are networking with your Top 50 folks. Make sure they like the way you are staying in touch with them.

Expanding Your Sphere of Influence

One of the benefits of becoming a motivated networker is that you are continually expanding your sphere of influence. This means that you are involved and have a say in how the world works – at least part of it. You have broader resources that you can draw upon when you need help. The more people you know and who know you will determine how many people show up at your funeral – or your 100th birthday – whichever comes first.

Let's bring back the image of those concentric circles now. What are the next rings that lie outside those of your Top 50 contacts? I propose that there are three more rings that we need to address here in our work together: Active, Lost and Future Networks.

Your Sphere of Influence

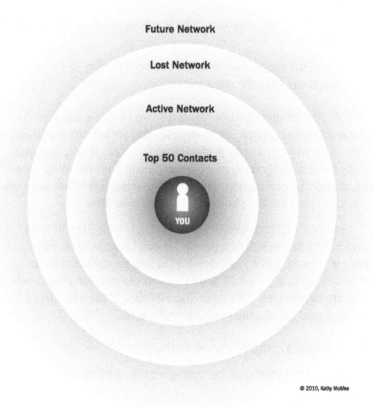

Future Network

Lost Network

Active Network

Top 50 Contacts

YOU

• Active Network. These are the people in your daily world. You live next door to them, you work with them and you see them at your meetings and gatherings. You may be friends, acquaintances or even arch-enemies. The point is, you run into them regularly. They are "active" in your life right now, and you have some kind of relationship with them. These are the easiest relationships to develop and strengthen from a networking point of view. Why? Proximity and regularity. You only have to extend yourself a little bit to start to build upon these relationships.

• Lost Network (also called the Past Network). These are the people who used to be in your active network, but something changed, and you haven't seen them in a very long time. You used to live next door to them, you were best friends in school, you worked on that project together at the old company, you socialized with them and then – something happened. Someone moved, someone got divorced, someone left the company, and you lost touch with that person. You haven't seen each other in a very long time. You may not even remember that person's full name. The good news is that you can reclaim your lost network by finding those individuals on the many social networking sites like Facebook®, LinkedIn®, Twitter™ and the thousands of other sites focused on connecting people online. Just recently, I was contacted by my best friend in middle school. It had been years since we were in touch with each other. It was a joy to hear about her life and family and her many adventures through the years. We can now pick up where we left off. This relationship may become important again in my life and business. Or it may just be a wonderful blast from the past. Either way, good stuff.

• Future Network. These are all the people you haven't yet met, but would like to. You may discover them purely by ac-cident and chance (the power of serendipity). Other people may suggest them as good contacts for you, or you might purposeful-ly seek them out through your networking activity. This is what I call "targeted networking." Think about whom you would like to add to your professional network right now. Whom would you like to have a relationship with that could add value to your life, career and business? Whose company would you enjoy and whom would you like to learn from? Whose brain would you like to pick? Write that person's name down .

If you are drawing a complete blank right now, don't worry; this is a normal reaction to this exercise. Why not get some ideas by flipping through a business magazine, newspaper or published list of people in your industry? Who are the movers and shakers in your field? Pick one, do your research on that person (that's easy these days thanks to the Internet and the social media sites). Now, find someone in your existing network (Top 50 or Active) who knows that person or knows someone else who knows that person who would be willing to introduce you. How do you make that happen? You tell everyone you know whom you are looking to meet.

A few years back I had the pleasure of conducting a series of two-day workshops called "Powerful Presentations." A number of executives from the insurance and financial services industries attended my course. They were all dynamic, talented and motivated leaders very willing to try new things to sharpen their presentation skills and confidence. One such leader was Alan. Shortly after the training workshop, Alan had a team presentation with the C-suite executives at his company, a leading global financial services organization. He and I had a private coaching session to strategize his team's approach. He committed to doing his Six Sigma® update presentation completely without PowerPoint®, using props and stories to enhance audience engagement.

Alan e-mailed me after his team presentation with the great news that it had gone extremely well. The CEO loved it and suggested that Alan and his team take this show on the road. Needless to say I was jumping up and down in my office after reading Alan's e-mail. At that moment I set the goal to meet the CEO of this large financial services organization.

For the next eight months, I told many people about my goal of meeting the CEO, not knowing who might know her or have connections to her. I did try the direct approach, asking Alan for an introduction, but that didn't materialize as I had hoped. Then I tried the cold-calling approach, telephoning the CEO's office and trying to get time with this very busy executive. Like most vendors, I was quickly referred to the HR department. No luck through this route.

I incorporated my goal of meeting this CEO into most every professional talk I gave about networking. I used it as an example of how the more specific you can be in who you are looking to meet, the closer you will get to reaching your goal. It wasn't until I sat down one day and had lunch with a wonderful woman in my Top 50 by the name of Judith. Judith at that time was on the staff of the YWCA. In the course of our conversation, I shared my goal about meeting this CEO and asked Judith if she knew her. She told me that she had lunch with her the week before. Wow! I was one degree away. Now I had to ask the big question: "Judith, do you think you could introduce me to her? I'd like to network with her and do more business with her company."

Judith said that she could do that, but suggested a better strategy. "Why don't we introduce you first to Liz, who used to work directly for the CEO and who is still very good friends with her? Liz is involved with some YWCA projects, as are you, and I think you two would hit it off. Liz can then introduce you to her."

I followed Judith's advice and got to know Liz, who, by the way, is a dynamic, talented, motivated and fun person. Liz is now part of my active network – a real bonus that I wasn't expecting to have in this journey!

Over the next two months, I had several face-to-face exchanges with Liz, getting to know her in the context of our board work together with the YWCA. She even purchased my audio CD program entitled "Motivated Networking Follow-up" that I was offering as a fundraising project for the non-profit organization.

I ran into Liz at the sponsor breakfast of the YWCA's Money Conference for Women. She enthusiastically came up to me at the breakfast buffet line and said, "I am so impressed with you. You're the reason I'm here today. Come sit down next to me." We had a great conversation over scrambled eggs and fruit. I then took a deep breath and asked her the question: "Liz, do you think you could introduce me to your CEO?" She responded by pounding her fist on the table and saying "Consider it done!"

Two months later the CEO, Liz and I were having lunch together in the company cafeteria. It was relaxed and interesting. As it turns out, the CEO is a very approachable and real person who happens to have a very big job. I followed up after that luncheon with a personalized card.

Three months later, I got an e-mail from an HR leader at the company telling me that she would like to speak to me about an executive coaching assignment. Upon probing, it turned out that the CEO had suggested my name. I landed the assignment and now have the opportunity once again to serve the company and its employees. Networking builds not only relationships, but real business opportunities!

What's the moral of this story? Decide who you want to add to your professional network, tell everyone in your active network whom you are looking to meet and then be ready when the opportunity presents itself. It will present itself if you are patient, flexible and have the ability and willingness to build strong, supportive relationships.

"Treasure your relationships, not your possessions."
-Anthony J. D'Angelo, founder of The Collegiate EmPowerment Company

4. RULES OF THE ROAD

The True Spirit of Networking

The roads are shared by many people in all types of vehicles: SUVs, sedans, sports cars, wagons, motorcycles, bicycles. We also share our roads with pedestrians and sometimes wildlife. We must observe the rules of the road in order to navigate safely and get where we all need to be.

The same holds true for networking, but the rules of the road are mostly unwritten. They include giving, sharing, caring and reciprocating.

Helping Others; Asking for Help

To me, this is the true spirit of networking. It is about helping others to solve problems and achieve their goals, professionally and personally. And, it's about asking for help from others. You too have problems and dreams that require attention and help. When you approach your networking with an attitude of helpfulness, you will accelerate your success and make faster and more meaningful connections with people.

Many people I know (mostly women) are excellent at helping others but lousy at asking for help for themselves. To be an effective networker, you must be able to do both: help others and ask for help for yourself.

My good friend Kim once complained to me that she always extended herself to others in networking, and there was never any reciprocation. To her it felt like a one-way giving street. I asked her, "So, how good are you at asking for help from others?" She was silent and gave me a look that told me, "You're right. I stink at that."

Let's face it, it takes a strong person to ask for help – to reach out to others and share gaps and needs that you might otherwise want to keep to yourself. In college I learned that the smartest students were the ones who asked for help, who looked for additional resources, human and otherwise. It took me quite a few semesters of struggling on my own to realize that I was surrounded by a wealth of resources. Sometimes the best way of helping yourself is asking for help from others. The key to asking for help in networking is knowing what you want and whom you are looking to meet. You must get fairly specific about this. And you must bring this up during your networking meetings and conversations. Your contacts can't read your mind, and if you don't bring the subject up, it may go unnoticed and unrealized. And whose fault is that?

Giver's Gain Philosophy

Dr. Ivan Misner, founder and chairman of the BNI® network, the self-proclaimed largest business networking organization and referral network, is credited for the "giver's gain" idea: You must give of yourself freely and without expectation of return for your giving. If you do this, good things will come your way. I call this the boomerang effect. Cast out good things in the world, and good things will come back to you, perhaps not immediately, but eventually. Send out negative energy and actions into the world, and you know what's coming back to you. Eventually, bad things come your way. You get what you give. You reap what you sow.

Law of Reciprocity

The law of reciprocity means to give and take mutually – to return in kind. It is often associated with the expression "You scratch my back, I'll scratch yours." When someone gives you something or does a kindness for you, you feel an internal obligation to repay the favor in some way. Giving and receiving favors are common daily exchanges among friends, which happen in every culture on earth.

Of course, the law of reciprocity is more carefully guarded when practiced in the context of business or politics, where "buying favors" can not only produce negative public opinion but sometimes legal consequences. Most companies have "gift policies" and discourage their employees, leaders and board members from receiving things of value from others. Even if the thing has no value, the act of receiving it may be misconstrued by others. It's something to be avoided at all costs. No company likes to deal with this sort of publicity embarrassment – it drives up PR costs and creates an unneeded company distraction.

So how do you resolve this issue when the very definition of networking is: the art of building and maintaining mutually-beneficial relationships before you need them? Giving, taking and exchanging are part of what happens when people who care about each other try to help each other. Is it really necessary to have our guard up all the time? Is it wise to avoid receiving favors from others because you don't want to feel obligated, guilty or beholden to anyone else?

I'd like to give you another way to think about this. Practice giving of yourself with no strings attached. Whether it's your time, money, knowledge or possessions, give without expectation of return. I know that this is a tough thing to do. We at least expect to get a thank you (verbal or written). But let that go too. Practice giving for the sheer love of it – because it makes you feel good. When you get good at that, then you are ready to practice receiving with grace. Allow other people to give to you because it brings them joy. Whether it is a compliment, treating you to lunch, giving you a book or some helpful advice, just receive it gracefully.

I have a dear friend named Gary. He was my very first boyfriend in high school (about a million years ago). He is married to a wonderful woman named Denise, and they have two lovely kids. Every Christmas, Gary and Denise send a small present to a group of 15 friends. Year after year, they send something inexpensive, but fun and spirited. Their gift makes us smile, and receiving Gary and Denise's gift has become part of our holiday tradition. I decided a long time ago that I was going to practice the act of receiving gracefully without the expectation of immediate reciprocation. I send a thank-you card and let them know that we received it and enjoyed it. But I don't rush off to the store to buy them something because I feel guilty. I just enjoy the good feelings of receiving someone's kindness. I believe that Gary and Denise do what they do because it brings them joy to give and to stay in touch with a small group of close life-long friends. (Don't you wish your first boyfriend had been this cool?)

In the context of networking, you must recognize the power of the law of reciprocity and how it affects you and others. You have the choice whether to let it dictate your feelings and behavior, or if you choose to create another experience for yourself. This leads me to another very cool idea.

The Pay It Forward Philosophy

The expression "pay it forward" is used to describe the concept of asking that a good turn be repaid, not to you directly, but to someone else in the future. It's the ultimate act of selfless kindness. It creates a cycle of good will that keeps on going.

Author Catherine Ryan Hyde wrote a book called Pay It Forward: A Novel, which was later turned into a movie featuring actors Kevin Spacey and Helen Hunt. She suggests that if someone does you a favor, something big, something you couldn't do on your own, and instead of paying it back, you paid it forward to three people, and the next day, each of them paid it forward to three more, and the day after, those 27 each paid it forward to another three, eventually, that would come to more than 4.7 million people. With these kinds of numbers, the world would soon start to change – for the better!

My networking friend David has a similar idea and passion. He started a regional executive roundtable group. David is very active on LinkedIn® and shares his leadership thoughts with executives who are going through the job search process. I first met David interviewing for a job at his company. I was overqualified for his marketing position and seeking more money than his budget allowed, so we didn't go forward with the employment relationship. Most people would walk away at this point, never contacting each other again. But there was some synergy between David and me and both of us stayed in touch during the next few years. David has called upon me to be a speaker at his Executive Roundtable events and to play an advisory role in his volunteer startup organization. He believes that every executive must adopt and practice a pay-it-forward philosophy. It's a leadership trait that creates positive energy, positive change and positive relationships in the world.

These are the rules of the road in networking. Practice them and your journey will be more rewarding than ever before.

"Service to others is the rent you pay for your room here on earth."
-Shirley Chisholm, the first African-American woman
to win a seat in the United States Congress (1924–2005)

5. ROAD GRIME AND DOOR DINGS

First and Last Impressions Count in Networking

How you present yourself when you network is very important. While I encourage you to be authentically you, I want you to present the best you possible. Everything matters, including how you look, how you act, your energy and your attitude – and yes, what you drive. It all says something about you. It all communicates.

This section is dedicated to helping you become more aware of your visual communication so that you can make a conscious choice to improve it and get a better outcome when you network with other people.

Malcolm Gladwell, in his book *Blink: The Power of Thinking Without Thinking*, established a theory that our decision-making is influenced not only by careful study of all the facts and information, but also by an unconscious, split-second processing of a few particular details. As quickly as you can blink your eye, most of us draw conclusions about people, and Mr. Gladwell contends that these first impressions or gut instincts about things are pretty much on target.

Additional support comes from the study of Neuro Linguistic Programming, the science of how you run your brain. NLP is based upon the idea that everything we think, feel and do is neurologically linked – every cell in our body is affected. The NLP Model of Communication suggests that we process external input through our senses and filter it through a variety of high-level individual filters. You can download an illustration of the NLP Model of Communication at ModernJedi.com/NLPmodel

This happens almost instantaneously, and we form an internal representation. We derive meaning from the external input, and that meaning shapes our thinking. That internal representation impacts your emotional state. It may make you feel happy, sad, silly, mad, annoyed, energized, etc. That particular emotional state triggers physiological responses. Your heart rate increases or slows down, your breathing changes, you widen your eyes or narrow the glance, your face flushes, you clench your fist or cross your arms. All of this happens almost unconsciously. What comes next is your outward behavior. You do or say something. And that impacts your outcome.

If you want a better outcome, then change your behavior. How do you do that? You can start by changing how you think, how you feel or what you do with your body. Make a small shift in any one of these, and the other two will follow. Neurological linkage at work; it's a beautiful design.

But it's not easy to control. Allan Pease, author of *The Definitive Book of Body Language*, asserts that "Our attitudes and emotions are continually revealed on our faces and we are completely unaware of it most of the time." We are so accustomed to doing what we do, without really thinking about it. We just respond; we react to what happens to us, and not always with the best outcome. By increasing your skills of observation and paying more attention to your physiology and that of others, a few very wonderful things can happen for you:

- You suspend judgment of yourself and others long enough to create a better outcome.

- You gain additional sensory information that could help you decide the best course of action.

- You are less likely to overreact to situations or jump to incorrect conclusions.

- You become more self-aware and in control of your behavior.

- You are more fully present, which allows you to build and maintain rapport with other people.

I call this body language intelligence. It is understanding and appreciating your original mobile communication device – your body. It goes everywhere you go and is constantly sending messages to other people. In networking situations, your body language will have a large impact on your ability to make strong connections with people.

Handshakes and Cell Phones

One of the first and last impressions that you make is with your handshake – the traditional greeting of hello and goodbye. The handshake serves to build trust between people as you bring someone into your personal space and press the flesh and exchange energy. The handshake is a powerful nonverbal communication. Usually it goes fairly well, but then sometimes you miss or mess up.

Dan had invited me to speak at his upcoming training workshop. I was recommended to him by my good friend Julie. I was not being paid for this speaking "gig" and was doing it as a favor for Julie. Dan asked me to meet him at a local breakfast café to discuss the event. When I arrived, Dan was already at the table and was talking on his cell phone. I approached him and he gave me a head nod, signaling to me that he was just finishing up his call. I sat down. When his call was done, he shook my hand, giving me one of those finger tip, princess handshakes that I hate so much. His energy was wired; he was noticeably jittery and spoke very fast. His eyes kept looking around the room, as if he were expecting someone else. He kept his cell phone on the table, and when it inevitably went off, he answered it again during our networking meeting. Another interruption. Our meeting was rushed and awkward, and I was starting to regret having said yes to this speaking engagement.

What went wrong? Dan's body language told me so much more than his words could. In just a short 15 minutes, Dan had put distance between us and set the tone for our relationship. I don't think he was aware of that, and I don't think that was his intention. Dan failed to adjust his body language to meet the energy level of his guest. He was wired; I was not (at least not at that particular moment). His cell phone behavior was perhaps the most offensive. I urge you to turn off your cell phones while networking or meeting with other people. The physiology of taking a call during a meeting is all wrong. Later on, I had the opportunity to share with Dan that I, like many professional women that I know, prefer a firmer handshake. "Treat me like your equal," I explained. He was surprised and told me that he shakes a woman's hand more gently out of respect for her. He learned this while growing up in his family. One of his female co-workers was in the room during this discussion, and she chimed in to agree with me. She said that she hated when men do that to her. This was a teaching moment for both of us. Dan got important feedback on how his handshake was received by women (at least two of us), and I learned more about Dan's background and intention. He wasn't such a rude guy after all; he just had limited exposure to professional businesswomen. We practiced shaking hands until he got it just the way I liked it.

There are three principles of a professional handshake:

1. Complete: You want to make full contact, that is web-to-web, with the groove between your index finger and your thumb coming together without any gaps in that space.

2. Equal: Make sure that both people's palms are in vertical position. Neither party should attempt to dominate or be submissive, which is communicated unconsciously when one hand is underneath or on top of the other person's palm. There should be no bending at the wrist.

3. Receptive: Apply the same pressure that you receive. You don't want to hurt someone with too much pressure. "Bone crushers" and "vice grips" should be avoided at all times. At the other extreme, you don't want to give them a wimpy grip. Hug the hand, by wrapping your fingers around their palm. The handshake should feel good to you both. It should never create physical pain or displeasure.

Power Up Your Professional Image

A big part of your visual impact is how you dress, how you groom yourself – your physical appearance. Many people I know are very self-conscious about their weight, yet they ignore other important aspects of their appearance. It's not just about your body size and shape; it's what you do with it. Fat, thin, young, old, tall, short – whatever configuration your body is, you can learn to leverage it to your advantage. You must pay attention to the details, and take steps to make the necessary enhancements.

No one likes to hear the complaints of a thin person, but let me share mine with you. Clothes hang off me. Nothing fits well. Hem lines from slacks that I buy in the store are always too long. The new waist lines drop lower on my hips, and I am uncomfortable with that look and fit. It gives me the appearance of having droopy drawers or that teen look that I have certainly outgrown. I hate high-heeled shoes as they are dreadfully uncomfortable (and dangerous) for me. I have a closet full of clothes and shoes that don't really work for me, and I am not alone. The majority of American women have the same problem. We wear only 20 percent of what's in our closet, but we keep buying, buying, buying. Is it a problem of retail therapy or a desperate attempt to find something that fits and looks good?

In 2009, I had the good fortune of meeting and networking with a woman named Janice, who is an unusual combination of financial planner and makeup artist. She has a side business with Mary Kay® Cosmetics as an independent beauty consultant. Despite having worked for Maybelline cosmetics for three years, I'm really not that much into makeup. But Janice struck me as an interesting person, a motivated woman – certainly worth getting together with for coffee. Deep down, I was worried that she would ask me to host a Mary Kay© home party – something I really didn't want to do. I was thinking of all the other ways in which I might be able to help her without having to host a party.

As a result of our first networking coffee, we launched a fabulous new program called Power Up Your Professional Image™, a professional development event-based company focused on helping career minded women get an edge in the workplace. Check it out at PowerUpYourProfessionalImage.com.

We have invited many service professionals to assist with this program as locally based delivery partners, including image consultants, wardrobe specialists, skin care and color cosmetic consultants, photographers, communication specialists, life coaches, even financial advisors. And the day is filled with networking opportunities, in a safe, supportive and invigorating environment.

As a result of being involved with these women, I realized that I needed to invest in my own professional image. I hired an image consultant to do a color analysis and a closet audit to determine what worked and what didn't. We weeded through my closet and donated about half of my possessions. That was a great investment of time and money. I then hired a tailor specializing in alterations for professional women, to custom alter my core remaining pieces, including suits, slacks, blouses and even sweaters. If it didn't fit, it didn't stay, including shoes. I re-examined my purchasing strategies and wardrobe priorities. I now value quality of clothing above quantity of clothing and am more committed to buying things that look good, fit well and last. Trendy fashion clothing that creates an instant retail thrill for me is out of style forever more.

In addition to this change in buying pattern, the Power Up initiative has led me to meet many connected women. I have gained valuable new insight and knowledge, and it has created a new revenue stream for my company. All of this value was created from one networking meeting over coffee. Yes, there is magic in networking; you just need to be open to it.

Attention to Detail

This part is perhaps the hardest for me to write, because I don't always practice what I preach in regard to keeping a clean car.

People make instant judgments about you based upon what you drive. Consider it automotive grooming, but an occasional car wash can go a long way in improving your professional image and sending the right signals to other people. Here's one time that I realized how important that was.

At a regional conference, I had met Jack Mitchell, the author of two books, *Hug Your Customers* and *Hug Your People*, and the CEO of the very successful high-end men and women's clothier Mitchells/Richards in Connecticut. Jack was the keynote speaker at the conference. (Hint: Always introduce yourself to the speaker and follow up. Speakers are usually very connected and interesting people.)

I reached out to Jack after the meeting. I also met his terrific executive assistant. He invited me down to his store in Westport, Connecticut, to discuss ideas and a possible collaboration. It was rather intimidating to think about what I was going to wear to this meeting. Jack's shoes probably cost more than my entire outfit, including jewelry and wedding ring! But I had the impression that Jack was a kind and down-to-earth person and that he would receive me well.

The meeting went well until the moment where Jack graciously offered to give me a box of his book *Hug Your Customers* and said that he'd bring them out to my car personally. This was a very gentlemanly thing to do. However, it sent me into a near internal panic as I could see in my mind's eye how filthy and unkempt my car was. I would have to open the trunk for him. What was in there? How dirty was my green car? Could you even tell it was the color green? What was strewn in the backseat that he might see? My briefcase, papers, clothing, hangers, maybe even dry cleaner plastic bags? This was going to be a killer last impression. I was sweating now. There was no wiggling out of this one.

In the end, I survived this professional image violation. Jack went on to hire me for a short engagement. If I could do it all over again, I might have taken 30 extra minutes to have my car washed. I would have cleaned out my stuff and made my vehicle a little more respectable – just in case.

Olfactory Offenses

How good do you smell? Do you smoke? Do you wear a lot of perfume or use heavily scented deodorant? Do you have coffee breath much of the time? All of these scents create strong first and lasting impressions, and most of the time they are negative. If you are a smoker, you need to be aware that the smell of cigarette smoke permeates your hair, clothing, car and anything you touch. It's like the cloud that followed Pig-Pen, the character from the Charles Schulz "Peanuts" cartoon.

Your particular habit and lifestyle choice may have a significant negative impact on your professional image, and most people won't tell you what they are thinking. Before you send me hate mail or put this book in the trash out of anger, please remember my intention is to help you be more professionally successful with networking and relationship-building. I also want you to live a full, healthy and rich life. Smoking is counterproductive to these goals.

For other bad smells, you need to take proactive action. Carry a toothbrush in your purse (carefully sealed of course); eat breath mints before meeting with people; rinse out your mouth with water more frequently (a suggestion from my dentist); pass up the perfume and go natural. (This is especially important when traveling on airplanes or attending conferences. Some people are highly allergic to perfumes.)

If you are meeting with people after a meal, you might want to watch how much garlic you eat. While excellent for your blood and health and absolutely delicious in my opinion, garlic will permeate your pores and you will smell of it. This might irritate other people who don't enjoy garlic or didn't partake of it that day. On the other hand, garlic will keep the networking vampires at a safe distance. These folks can suck the living daylights out of your professional network.

"There are four ways, and only four ways, in which we have contact with the world. We are evaluated and classified by these four contacts: what we do, how we look, what we say, and how we say it."
-Dale Carnegie, author of *How to Win Friends and Influence People*,
1937

CHECKLIST #1

Good work. You are on your way. You've completed Part I of your networking journey. Part II will introduce you to several important techniques that will enhance your networking skill and confidence. When you have completed these affirmations and actions, you will be ready for Part II.

☐ I am prepared to push myself out of my comfort zone to meet new people and build new professional relationships.

☐ I am willing to spend the necessary time, money and energy to get more organized and disciplined about networking so that I can effectively incorporate it into my daily routine.

☐ I have completed the My World Exercise™ (download template at NetworkingAhead.com) and know who is in my current network by name.

☐ I understand who is in my Top 50 contact list and am prepared to invest more in these relationships with a greater frequency of touch and higher quality of communication.

☐ I have practiced and gotten external feedback on my handshake. It is neither too soft nor too hard, but achieves the three qualities of a professional handshake: complete, equal and receptive.

PART II

START DRIVING
PREPARING FOR
NETWORKING SUCCESS

6. GO THE SAME SPEED

How to Build Rapid Rapport When Networking

Imagine that you are on the highway, and you're racing along, passing all the cars one by one. You are on a mission, determined to get where you are going, or perhaps you are enjoying yourself, and the speed takes on a life of its own. Whatever the motivation, you are passing a lot of people, until you see those flashing lights in your rear view mirror. Busted.

I remember once when this happened to me in Massachusetts. I was late for a coaching session with a client in Boston. I had to make up some time, so it was more "pedal to the metal" driving faster than I normally do. I became obsessed with getting away from a very large truck that was on the road, fearing it might accidentally throw windshield-breaking rocks my way. The police officer didn't say much; in fact, he didn't show me much attention or respect at all. He just wrote me that $210 ticket and left me there talking to myself. He wasn't in the mood to listen to a bunch of excuses, nor was he interested in building rapport and getting to know me, another out-of-state speeder in his book. He was just doing his job.

When I shared this news with my husband, he reminded me of two important things. First, the car does have cruise control, and this would help me keep a constant speed on the open highway. Cruise control also improves gas mileage and efficiency and is less demanding physically on the driver. He also shared a sensible strategy with me: If you can help it, try not to be out in front of the other cars by any great distance. Keep with the pack. This way you are protected. A police officer would have to pull over all the cars in your cluster, and this would be difficult to do.

Speeding Tickets Are Also Given in Networking

This advice is also pertinent to networking. When you talk too fast or move too fast when networking with a person of a different style and speed, you push that individual away without even knowing it or intending it. Visually dominant people tend to be fast talkers. They often don't even finish their sentences because they are moving on to another topic. They see in pictures, sometimes movies. They are rapid processors of information.

Now imagine what happens when a visually dominant person meets with a more relaxed, more methodical kinesthetically dominant person. These folks like to be comfortable, they feel things, they reflect, they speak more slowly. When you mix a visual person with a kinesthetic person, you can often get a painful mismatch of styles unless one or both of you know how to be flexible and know how to pace to lead.

Pace to Lead

This is a simple and powerful concept that you can learn to do and apply in almost any business or personal situation. It doesn't require any fancy training, just a high level of awareness of what's going on in the moment. If you want to connect and build rapport with someone, then you need to let him or her set the pace and lead for the first few minutes. You want to observe that person's body language and vocal pacing and match it. If the individual is sitting back in a chair in a relaxed fashion and speaking quietly and slowly, you want to start off this way as well. Make a conscious effort to be at his or her speed, even if you are excited, enthusiastic and pumped up with caffeine. Purposely slow down and follow the other person's lead.

The beautiful thing about building rapport with others is that the connection is made largely at an unconscious level. You feel good about others and are comfortable with them. Sometimes you get the feeling that you've met them before. You are starting to like these people, and likability is a key factor in business and professional success. You have created a foundation from which the conversation can flow and a relationship can develop. This is a solid base from which trust can begin to develop through time.

In a matter of moments, you can build rapid rapport with others. Soon they will begin to follow your lead. You will know that you have rapport with them when you begin to lead and move into your natural speed and style and they follow.

Mismatching Body Language and Energy Levels

I had met Jack through my local chamber of commerce. He had heard me speak at a seminar at our local library that offers a fantastic business program series. Jack called me and invited me to meet him for coffee to discuss some business opportunities he was developing. He indicated that he might want to hire me as a marketing consultant. I was excited to hear more as Jack might become a new (paying) client. When Jack and I sat down for coffee, I quickly became engaged and eager to learn more. My brain went into full brainstorming mode. My mouth quickly followed, spurting out all sorts of ideas. Jack sat back in his chair and I assumed he was taking in all of this incredible free marketing advice. I came up with one brilliant suggestion that he immediately applied that afternoon with a new prospect and landed a new piece of business. Jack shared this success with me on the telephone. I knew at that moment that I had the consulting assignment in the bag. I had just demonstrated my value.

Surprisingly, Jack selected the other marketing consultant, not me. When I asked him why, he said that he felt that the other guy was a better fit for him and his business needs. I was shocked and stunned. How much more did he need to see clearly that I could help him accelerate his business? The truth was that Jack didn't need more; he needed less from me. During my networking meeting with him, I completely misread his body language signals, ignored important verbal clues and unconsciously went into hyper-Kathy mode. I was fast talking, overpowering with my energy and overly demonstrative. I was more than Jack could handle. I failed to build rapport with Jack in a way that he was comfortable with. I exhausted him.

Has that ever happened to you? If so, consider what outcome might have been possible if you had exercised a little more awareness and self-control. It doesn't take much effort to adjust your energy level in the initial moments of the conversation so that the other person is more comfortable with you. Mirroring and matching techniques and rapport building skills can work to get you better service in restaurants, banks and retail stores. It also works effectively on the telephone.

It's More than Just Words that Count

When you are face to face with people, 38 percent of the meaning that they take away from your communication is influenced by "paralinguistic" factors or your tone of voice, according to UCLA Professor Albert Mehrabian. His well-renowned and often-quoted study conducted in the 1970s is referred to as the "7%-38%-55% Rule." This means your communication in face-to-face situations is influenced by:

- 7% verbal: the actual words that are spoken;

- 38% vocal: the way the words are said (tone of voice);

- 55% visual: what the listener sees you do when you speak, including your visual appearance, your facial expressions and your body language.

This theory is useful in explaining the importance of meaning, as distinct from words. Understanding the difference between words and meaning is a vital capability for effective communications and relationships. And it starts in those first few minutes of getting to know someone.

Matching Vocal Patterns

I'd like to introduce you to your vocal dashboard. It is a very cool and powerful instrument panel that gives you more control and more influence when you use your voice. We all have a vocal dashboard, but most of us set it and forget it, never adjusting the dials to leverage the power that our voices truly possess.

Consider the words of Arthur Samuel Joseph, author of *Voice of a Leader: Vocal Awareness to Empower Your Communication in Business and Life*, "You make your living through your voice. Your mouth is not just your mind out loud."

Rather than just talking, consider playing with the knobs on your vocal dashboard to power up your communication. Developing greater mastery over your voice is not just a skill reserved for singers, actors and professional speakers. It is for anyone who wants to be heard, has something to say and could use a little more influence in his or her life. That includes you.

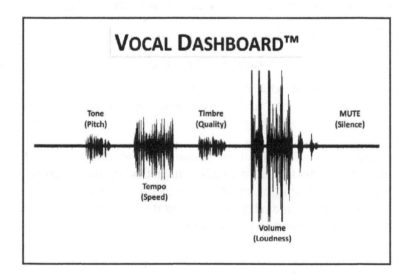

Let's examine the five basic dials on your vocal dashboard:

1.   **Tone** of your voice (pitch)

2.   **Tempo** of your voice (speed)

3.   **Timbre** of your voice (quality)

4.   **Volume** of your voice (loudness)

5.   **Mute** (the powerful sound of silence)

Expand Your Tonal Range

Think of a professionally trained singer, one who can hit high notes and low notes. Now think of someone you know who has an annoyingly high-pitched voice and never wavers from it. Now think of what you sound like when you are giving a command to your dog, and you really want the little darling to listen to you. You probably lower your voice and use an authoritative and commanding voice. These are all examples of tone or pitch. We all have a range. The goal is to use the full range of our tone, and select the pitch that will work best for the particular outcome we desire at that moment.

The Good and Bad of Upspeak

Upspeak is what happens when a person makes a question out of a sentence that isn't a question. It is the result of lifting your tone or pitch at certain parts of the sentence. Upspeak is a common affliction for teenagers, some women and younger professionals. Upspeak can put doubt in the listener's mind and can cause that person to think that you don't know what you are talking about. If you are overusing the upspeak tonality, you may be negatively chipping away at your professional credibility.

Jack Griffith, author of *How to Say It® at Work*, suggests that we avoid ending declarative sentences in a rising note. This is a verbal bad habit more common to women than men. It makes a statement sound tentative, even doubtful, as if the speaker were continually seeking approval.

To better understand what upspeak sounds like, watch the short television interview with me and Steve Adubato at MotivatedSpeaker.com (visit the Press Room to view the videos).

You can use upspeak strategically to your advantage. There will be times when you want to introduce doubt in people's minds. For example, you might say, "Is this solution good enough?" (Lifting your voice on the word "enough.") Or even use it with a statement such as, "This is the best we can do." (Lifting the voice on the words "best" or "do.")

You can also leverage upspeak to gain agreement from people if you accompany it with a positive head nod. For example: "You like this?" (Nodding the head and lifting the voice on the word "this.") This technique is one that you'd have to practice a great deal. There is sales power when you can get the prospect's head bobbing.

Tempo: The Metronome of Your Speech

You may not realize it, but you have control over how quickly or how slowly you speak. You'll want to be careful not to talk too fast with someone who has a slower pace of speech. If you desire to build rapport with this person, you must step out of your normal speech pattern and purposefully slow down your communication. When you get practiced at this, you'll discover that you can apply this powerful technique to many different situations, including those outside of networking. For example, if you are giving a public speech or presentation, you'll want to slow down your normal conversational pace by 20 percent. You can also make yourself a more interesting speaker by varying the tempo of your delivery throughout your presentation, speeding up and slowing down among different thoughts and ideas. This variation in tempo can serve to hold your audience's attention. Remember that monotone voices can put audiences to sleep almost as fast as too many boring PowerPoint® slides.

Probably the bigger challenge is for a normally slow talker to speed it up in order to build rapport with someone new. This can be physically tiring for them. However, the duration that you need to sustain this unusual activity will be brief, perhaps two to three minutes. Once you have established rapport, you can use your body language and your vocal patterns to slow down and open up the other person and bring the conversation to a place where you are more comfortable. This is the art of pacing to lead. If you do it well, you eventually get to lead.

Quality May Vary

You don't have to have a beautiful voice in order to be effective in leveraging it to build relationships. Quality or timbre, as it is referred to vocally, has many different aspects to it. You can strive to be clear as a bell and enunciate every consonant in every word, creating a formal speech sound effect. While this creates the impression of being articulate and perhaps highly educated, you may unconsciously be pushing certain people away from you. If this sounds like you, here's what you can do that maintains your high standards, but utilizes flexibility for the sake of building rapport with others. Try adding more texture to your voice. Think of when you have a head cold or a stuffy nose. You get that radio voice that other people find sexy and attractive. Sometimes a raspy quality to the voice makes it stand out and makes it somewhat endearing. You can learn to adjust the timbre of your voice in certain situations while still maintaining your authenticity and personal values. Be careful not to make your change in timbre too obvious or extreme. You don't want to come off as a bad actor. Practice on the telephone, matching the texture of the caller's voice.

It Sounds as if You're Not from Around Here

This brings up the topic of heavy accents and regional vocal traits. In addition to building rapport with others, we want to be understood easily. As the listener, we want to be careful not to judge people quickly or make them feel like an outsider. I remember living and working in Europe for three years. No matter how hard I tried to speak the British version of the English language, there's wasn't a week that went by without some stranger asking me, "So, what part of America are you from?" This always made me feel like an outsider and not really welcomed.

If you are someone who was born in a different country from the one where you are now living, you probably experience this vocal alienation effect even more than I did. Here are a few ideas that you might want to consider:

- Be patient and forgiving of others. Perhaps their exposure to the world is different from yours. You can help to educate them gently and work together to build a bridge of understanding, tolerance and racial justice.

- Slow down your speech, and select words that you can confidently and clearly enunciate. If there are words that you use that trip you up or confuse other people, find a substitute. Simple words are best for communication.

- Consider working with an accent modification coach. Erica Walch is the founder of SpeakEasyEnglish.com. Her company, located in Springfield, Massachusetts, offers both in-person training and distance training for foreign-born professionals who need or want to modify their accent for the sake of clearer communication in English. I consider this type of professional development a career investment and one that shows tremendous motivation and awareness of yourself and your impact on others. To be an effective communicator, sometimes you need to do more than learn to read, write and speak a different language.

Can You Turn That Thing Down?

People are pretty sensitive to volume. My client Sharon told me that she keeps an extra bottle of aspirin in her desk drawer at work because her boss speaks so loudly. It gives her a headache; the volume creates physical pain for her. I imagine her boss is unaware of this negative effect she is having on a key member of her staff.

Other people speak so softly that they are hard to hear. You have to strain to take in what they are saying. Unless you are the big chief in the room and people are highly motivated (if not required) to listen to you, speaking too softly all the times can reduce your influence and communication effectiveness.

Giving Women a Voice

I have found that women, in particular, struggle with increasing the volume of their voices. Most of us were raised to be pleasant, cooperative and quiet. Ladies don't raise their voices. This would be unladylike. Worse yet, we say nothing. We hold our tongue when really we have opinions and information that would bring value to the table. The other travesty about women and voice is that we don't use our voices when we really need them to protect ourselves.

My training as a martial artist has taught me that my voice is one of my greatest defense weapons. There is a fundamental difference between screaming (usually in a high pitch and from the throat) and yelling from the diaphragm. In the martial art of Tae Kwon Do, we are taught the *kihup* (pronounced key-up). This is the shout or yells Tae Kwon Do students make when they do their kicks and punches. It's important to *kihup* with spirit and volume. It actually gives you extra physical power and has the effect of intimidating your attacker. This vocal technique is one of the first things we teach women when we conduct women's self-defense workshops. Some women are very uncomfortable doing this. They are not used to raising their voices. It scares them. If you are a woman reading this book right now, or if you have a wife, daughter, mother, girlfriend or female colleague, please share this with them.

The Power of Silence

Perhaps my favorite dial on the vocal dashboard is the mute button. You know – the button on your telephone that you press when you don't want anyone on the conference call to hear the sounds of your multi-tasking. All kidding aside, finding your mute button when you are communicating with people in person is a powerful discovery. There is power in the sound of silence. It creates space for people to consider what you have said. You don't have to fill every moment with new thoughts and ideas. What usually happens in this instance is that you fill them with comfort words like "Um" and "ah" and "so." Try saying nothing for a few seconds. Purposely say inside your head, "Now stop talking." Sit quietly and observe what's going on. Be comfortable and confident in this strategic break. Something magical may happen next. The other person may speak up and give you new information that you wouldn't have garnered if you hadn't made space for it to come out in the open.

There is a difference between awkward silence that makes people uncomfortable and purposeful silence that engages people on a conscious and unconscious level. You'll figure out the difference, but I want you to get comfortable even with the discomfort of silence. It always serves a purpose. It's like breathing; you couldn't live without it.

"People don't do business with you because you're a geek and can do regression in your head. They come to do business with you because they like you."
-James Lee of Chase Manhattan Bank (1997)

7. MY WAY OR THE HIGHWAY

Express Your Personal Brand When You Network

Like it or not, the car you drive says something about you. It is an expression of your personal brand. And just as there are many different styles, makes, models and colors of cars, there are that many different kinds of networking styles. The only thing that is important is that your style works for you. You must expect it to be different from other people's style. There is no right or wrong way to network (although there is some basic etiquette you need to adhere to; see Chapter 9, "No Tailgating"). What really matters is that you do it – build relationships in your professional network.

What Is a Personal Brand?

We live in a branded world. Brands influence our buying decisions. We have relationships with brands – emotional attachments. We trust some and dislike others. They mean something to us: good, bad and sometimes indifferent. They promise us something, and we expect them to live up to this every time. As rational and logical as we think we are, we are affected by brands in a deeply personal and emotional way.

The same holds true for people. We all have a personal brand and whether you know it or not, you already have one. It's encapsulated in your image, your identity, your reputation. It's the unspoken promise that you make to the world, what people expect from you. The question is: Are you fully leveraging your personal brand?

The goal of a brand is to gain real estate in the gray matter of people's brains and the soft tissue of their hearts. We want you to think of us and love us so much that you choose us, prefer us over others and recommend us often. Your personal brand needs to create a distinctive, ownable position in someone's mind.

How Do You Do This?

It starts by being true to yourself. It's very difficult to hold up a façade for long periods of time. Quite frankly, it's exhausting. And while we all need to improve things and correct shortcomings, the strength of our personal brand lies in our natural strengths, talents, passions and even our quirks.

Personal branding expert Rahna Barthelmess suggests that your personal brand is your signature for success. She believes that if you know your personal brand, develop it and manage it consistently, then you have the opportunity to do only the work that you love for the rest of your life. "Living your personal brand should be as natural as breathing," states Rahna. It's something you do every second of every day.

Here are the questions that Rahna suggests you reflect upon to discover your personal brand:

1. How would you describe yourself? List as many adjectives or qualities that you can think of. Ask other people to add to this list.

2. What are you really good at?

3. What do you like about yourself?

4. What don't you like about yourself?

5. Identify the major skills that you have.

6. What parts of your current work do you like and why?

7. What parts of your current work do you not like and why?

8. What are you really passionate about – what do you love to do?

9. What is your current work style?

10. What values do you hold dear professionally? Personally?

Taking time to answer these questions is a start to discovering your personal brand. You may wish to read more on this topic. Subscribe to Rahna's blog at RahnaBarthelmess.com.

Express Your Personal Brand When You Network

When you engage in networking, you are primarily representing yourself, even if you work for a certain company. People are first connecting with you, the human being. Whom you work for is part of what you bring to the table in networking, but it's not the entire thing. Your employment is only one element of your packaging. The real product is on the inside – and that's you!

How to Become More Fluid and Natural in Networking

The secret to becoming more comfortable with networking is the same secret that will increase your success. It's called being authentically you. You must bring your whole human being to the table, not just the working-stiff part of you. Of course, some people won't like you, and that's OK. You don't have to be best friends with everyone.

If you allow yourself to be true, honest and real, then you will more easily attract the people who are meant to be in your life. You will naturally repel the others who do not align well with your values and personality.

Dump the Duds

Not everyone you meet in the course of networking is going to be a great connection for you. You will have ideal connections and duds and a lot of people somewhere in the middle.

Identifying the duds is important because they will not bring out the best in you. They will waste your time, suck out your life force and leave you with a taste of negativity for the whole process of networking. And we don't want this to happen, do we?

I was inspired by the concept of "dump the duds" after reading Michael Port's *Book Yourself Solid: The Fastest, Easiest, and Most Reliable System for Getting More Clients Than You Can Handle Even if You Hate Marketing and Sales*. Much of what Mr. Port talks about could be easily applied to networking rather than sales and marketing.

In his first chapter, entitled "The Red Velvet Rope Policy," Mr. Port suggests that we "dump the duds." That is, identify who doesn't make a good fit for you and purposefully let them go. I think this strategy is equally important in the networking process as well.

I'm thinking of one gentleman who was introduced to me by a mutual business associate. We got along well initially, and he eventually hired me to help him launch a new business venture. After working closely with him for a few months, we both discovered that we had very different styles and different values. We mutually agreed to discontinue our professional work together. We haven't spoken in a number of years. He is still on my e-mail list, but neither of us is ready to reconnect.

Upon reflection, I am grateful for this experience and for him for several reasons:

1. I discovered what a dud client for my business looks like. I'm sure I was a dud for him too. No doubt, we are ideal clients for someone else, just not each other.

2. I met other people through him, and these people have turned out to be beneficial in my life.

3. I had the chance to test drive my very first motivational talk at one of his events. The filming of this talk turned into a number of videos that I posted on YouTube.com that have reached thousands of people around the globe. The value chain continues.

Perhaps some connections are better off as networking contacts rather than clients. The relationship and expectations certainly change when money is exchanged. But underneath it all is the relationship. A strong one will withstand bumps in the road. A weak one will collapse under misunderstanding and conflict. Some connections are a misfit from the start.

The best approach in networking is to be you. Bring your authentic self into the networking relationship from the get-go. This way both of you will have the chance to see if this relationship will go anywhere. If it's not a fit, it's still a touch-point. You don't have to develop every networking connection into a mutually beneficial relationship. Be careful not to over-invest in dud clients and dud networking contacts. Move on and find those who complement your personal brand and goals.

"Be more of yourself, and less of everybody else!"
-Dan Schawbel, Managing Partner of Millennial Branding, LLC

8. CONSTRUCTION ZONE

How to Perfect Your Pitch and Leverage Purposeful Small Talk

Everybody wants good roads, but no one likes driving through a construction zone. You have to slow way down, wait in line for some guy with a Slow/Stop sign to wave you on. You didn't plan for this, and now you might be late. When the construction is complete, no one notices and life returns to normal.

To become effective in networking, there is some construction that you'll need to endure. You need to learn how to position yourself quickly (in 30 seconds or less), how to strike up a conversation with someone you haven't met before and quickly find common ground, and how to move around to meet more people without being uncomfortable or looking like you are "working the room."

I call this process learning to "perfect your pitch." It involves the skill of introducing yourself in such a way that the other person asks you more questions and invites you to talk more. It's learning how to ask questions of others to learn more about them. These conversations are the beginnings of potential relationships. It's the stage where you get to know something about the other person, decide if you like that individual and if he or she is interesting enough for a follow-up.

It is critical in this phase that you do not attempt to transact with this new person. Trying to sell your product or service at this startup phase of networking would severely shortchange the long-term potential of the relationship. Most people can smell a sales pitch from several yards away, and most people will immediately put their guard up toward you. Networking game over or at least penalty points issued.

I'd like you to repeat the networking mantra "Think relationships, not transactions; Think conversations, not sales pitches."

When networking with people for the first time, I encourage you to suspend the urge to interact with new people. This includes presenting your résumé or curriculum vitae unless they specifically ask for it. Instead, I want you to embrace the idea of purposeful small talk.

Purposeful Small Talk

Now small talk is synonymous with chitchat, idle or trivial conversation. It is usually associated with the light informal conversation for social occasions such as, "We stood around making small talk until the guest of honor arrived." The *small* in this expression alludes to unimportant subjects of conversation, as opposed to serious or weighty ones. Most people tolerate small talk as part of civility, but few people I know actually enjoy it.

So how do you put more "purpose" into your small talk? How do you make this type of conversation more meaningful without having to get overly heavy or intense too quickly?

You find common ground. You make yourself approachable by putting a smile on your face. You get out of your own head and take more interest in other people. You realize that purposeful small talk is nothing more than an icebreaker to warm up the conversation so that you might have a shot at getting to know this person and possibly helping them (or vice versa).

Here's an example. I recently attended a special event hosted at the Connecticut General Assembly Legislative Office Building in Hartford. I didn't know much about the event, but I needed to be there to attend a YWCA committee meeting following the event. I came from another appointment and arrived early. They were just finishing setting up the event. Now I had a choice. I could "mingle" in a near-empty room, or I could hide in the cafeteria, pretending to be busy looking at my BlackBerry®. I defaulted to the latter, but found it most unsatisfying, mostly because there were a few folks in the cafeteria who were having very loud conversations with their laptops (some sort of live meeting software). Frustrated with this forced eavesdropping (you couldn't not hear it), I elected to pay a visit to the ladies room.

Wouldn't you know it, there were two other businesswomen in the bathroom. These two were changing clothes and seemed in a hurry. The room was a bit hot and they were fanning themselves. I made a comment, telling them that the bathroom was indeed warm, but that the main lobby was much cooler. By asking another question, I learned that these two women had just set up the big display for the event.

When I moved into the main lobby, more people were starting to arrive for the event. I noticed one of the women from the bathroom was starting to greet guests. I walked over to her and commented how she cleaned up well and looked great in her white ruffled blouse and black pant suit. I introduced myself. Her name was Katherine and she was the executive director for the Connecticut Women's Hall of Fame. This was her event. We had a lovely conversation, I learned more about her organization and I told her a little about myself and what I did for a living. She expressed sincere interest; in fact, she commented, "Oh, I could really use your services."

Katherine introduced me to a few other guests who were arriving. We exchanged business cards. She invited me to attend their special event in November. I could see from the way she handled herself that Katherine was a woman of influence. She knows people. People know her. I'd like to meet more of her contacts. (Note to self: Follow up and get to know Katherine.)

What starts off as small talk can indeed lead to new possibilities. What makes small talk useful is when there is a bigger intention beyond it. Purposeful small talk helps you warm things up and can produce more mutually beneficial relationships. That, my friend, is one of the primary goals in networking.

What Makes a Good Networking Introduction?

Few people I know enjoy giving their 30-second elevator pitch. It can be one of the most aerobic parts of your day: heart pounding, palms sweating, inner dialogue on haywire. And that starts happening about 10 minutes before you have to say word one.

To calm yourself down and reduce the anxiety about the whole thing, I suggest you tell yourself that "This is just practice." With everyone to whom you introduce yourself or give your networking introduction, tell yourself you are just practicing. This type of communication is so fluid and flexible and forgiving! Give yourself a break, and lighten up on the pressure. Try to breathe.

The goal of your networking is to position yourself and to get the other person's permission to talk more. If you hear that individual reply, "Tell me more" or "That's interesting, how do you do that?" you have done well. Creating curiosity, interest and rapport is a key outcome that you should seek when you introduce yourself in networking situations.

The best networking introductions do five things really well. I call these the "MR ABE" criteria. If you can learn to dial up these five elements of your elevator pitch, you will be moving forward toward greater networking confidence and results:

M = memorable

R = relatable or relevant

A = authentically you

B = believable and credible

E = engaging and energized

Let's examine each one of these points, and figure out how we can construct your elevator pitch with these elements in place.

(For a free workbook to help you craft your elevator pitch, go to http://motivatednetworker.com/seminars/perfect-your-pitch/free-15-page-workbook/.)

Make Yourself More Memorable

You meet many people in the course of your life. Some stand out; some don't. Some people's names you can remember; others you don't. You, my friend, want to strive to be one of those memorable people. To do this, you must seek to be sticky. By this, I mean that you must find something about you (positive) that people can easily remember. Many people are visual and will link your face to your name. Others may remember you based upon something compelling that you said or did (again, hopefully positive).

Your challenge is to decide ahead of time how you want to be remembered. What do you want to "stick?" Is it your name? Is it your occupation? Is it your personal passion?

Here's the deal with stickiness and memory. If you attempt to tell your whole life story or every detail about everything you do, offer or have, nothing will stick. You must focus and be purposeful.

If you have a difficult-to-pronounce name, you might want to teach people how to say it. If they are unsure about how to pronounce your name, they will avoid it altogether. It's too awkward and uncomfortable. So, give them an easy way to remember you name. Here are two examples.

I met a woman whose name was Cauna. She said it quickly and I looked at her business card, but it didn't stick. I was suddenly uncomfortable with asking her for her name (again). We got into a discussion about teaching people how to pronounce your name, and she shared this with me: "My name is Cauna, pronounced like Kona coffee." I instantly smiled as I conjured up images of Hawaii and the delicious taste of Kona coffee. Cauna has anchored her name on something very positive and stimulated a multiple sensory experience for me in an instant. I followed up by sending her a card with a picture of coffee beans. I will always remember her and say to myself, "Cauna, like the Kona coffee."

Now, Cauna is a trust officer with a bank. She is not in the coffee business. But this doesn't matter. What does matter is that I can now confidently pronounce her name and will remember her. She has made it easier for me to get to know her.

How Can You Be More Relevant?

People don't listen to you until you have captured their attention. This holds true for parents, teachers, bosses and networkers. Even if you have a position of authority, you will experience a difference between people who hear you, listen to you and engage with you. The key is how relevant you are to them, and how much they can relate to you and you can relate to them. I like to define relevance as "I need you right now." In fact, I often ask myself this key question when thinking about connecting with my clients and prospects: "How can I be more relevant?"

In networking, relevance is what happens when people connect to what you are saying, because they can relate to it. You have found common ground and now have more to talk about.

Here's a fun approach to practice in a more formal networking setting, like chambers of commerce meetings. Before you say your name, ask a question. Get the people to go inside themselves and answer the question (or relate to the problem/experience you have just opened with).

Need a few examples of how this works?

- Anyone here have a messy desk? My name is Linda and I'm a professional organizer. I help busy professionals and business owners reclaim time and space in their lives and businesses by creating organizational systems that work for them. Linda – your professional organizer.

- Do you remember the "Peanuts" cartoon where Lucy, Linus and Charlie Brown are in the classroom? You never see the teacher, but you know that she's there because when she speaks, the kids hear (audience will answer "wha, wha, wha"). My name is Tammy and I'm a marketing consultant. I help business professionals like you take the blah-blah-blah out of your marketing speak. Tammy – your marketing consultant.

- When was the last time you sat through a really boring PowerPoint presentation? How excruciating was it? My name is Kathy and I'm an executive presentation coach. I help business professionals reduce their PowerPoint clutter so that they better engage their audience and move them to action. Kathy – your executive presentation coach.

The beauty of this approach is that you say your name only after you have their attention. They are more likely to remember your name and pay attention to what you have to say. This is a creative way to become more relevant when you introduce yourself in networking situations.

Authenticity Means Being Comfortable in Your Own Skin

How much conviction do you have in what you are saying? If the level is high, then your physiology or body language will back you up. Your nonverbal and verbal communication will be congruent. If your conviction is low – if, for example, you don't like the company that you work for, but you are forced to give the company "shpiel" – then your body language will give you away instantly. You will not come across as being comfortable in your own skin.

Have you ever witnessed this situation? Someone is talking about what he or she does for a living, and the conversation is pretty matter-of-fact. Then suddenly that person comes alive and gets animated, sharing with you something he or she is passionate about – perhaps a special project, a charity, an issue.

That person's entire physiology shifts as he or she becomes totally transformed with passion and energy. What just happened? (And how do we make this happen earlier in the conversation, interview or meeting?)

By sharing what you are passionate about when you network, the chances of a stronger connection increase substantially. You bring your entire human being to the party, not just the working-stiff part. I encourage you to share more of yourself when you network. Now, of course, there are topics that may be a bit dangerous (religion, politics, sex). Perhaps these topics are best put on hold until a deeper relationship is established.

William Shakespeare wrote, "To thine own self be true." This is a great philosophy when it comes to personal branding and to expressing your personal brand when you network with others.

If you attempt to be something or someone that you are not, or try to put on a professional façade when networking, you will quickly become exhausted and discovered. Your body language will give you away. Strive to be more authentic you when you network, and watch how this improves your conversations, connections and relationships!

Believability: Are You the Real Deal?

The flip side of the authenticity coin is believability. How credible are you? Do you look, sound and act the part? If you are a health coach, then showing up drinking a Coca-Cola® and eating a donut may send a mixed message.

You can't control what other people think, but you can influence it. When networking, don't brag, but remember to let people know about your experiences and credentials. Sometimes these are best showcased through client stories. Talk about whom you have worked with and what kind of problems you helped them solve. This will get the wheels turning in other people's heads about what value you can create for them and others they know.

Have someone else introduce you, and let them brag about you. This is the power of PR and third-party endorsement. You can maintain your modesty and humbleness while being positioned as an accomplished person.

The other aspect to consider when dialing up your credibility is your visual and vocal presentation. How you dress and how you use your voice will either build you up or break you down in other people's eyes. Human beings form judgments about other people in a blink of an eye. Your credibility and believability may be well served by powering up your professional image: polished shoes, clean fingernails, underwear that remains under your clothes, shirts and blouses that don't distract with too much skin showing, clothes that actually fit your body (tailoring is a great investment in your professional image).

Start paying more attention to how you end your sentences. Your voice inflection will communicate whether you are asking, stating a fact or commanding someone to do something. There will be times when you'll want to use all three of these voice inflection techniques.

You can put more confidence and authority into your voice by learning how to use the "low and slow" command tonality. Lowering the pitch of your voice (within your natural range) has other added benefits. It has the effect of slowing you down, thereby encouraging the more precise articulation of each word. It also tends to minimize any nasal vocal quality, which many listeners find annoying.

- Statement: Word ➡ Word ➡ Word (all words spoken with same emphasis)

- Question: Word ➡ Word ➚ Word (last word ends on a higher pitch note)

- Command: Word ➡ Word ➘ Word (last word spoken with lower tone of voice)

Engaging Means You Bring a Positive Life Force to the Conversation

Many people have some anxiety around the topic of networking (similar to public-speaking fears). As a result, their energy levels are diminished or altered in some unfavorable way. And people feel your energy. It either attracts them toward you or repels them away from you. Sometimes the impact is neutral, with no major gravitational pull either way. This doesn't help your networking efforts.

It's time to put more energy into your networking. It starts with your attitude and how you are thinking. Brain research continues to prove that we are all neurologically wired. What we think impacts how we feel, and that impacts our physiology and what goes on with our bodies. Change any one of these forces (thoughts, feelings, physiology), and you affect the other two.

This is why laughter can make such a big difference in your life. You are changing your physiology, which alters your state and shifts your mindset. It is also very contagious – in a positive way!

The next time you network, try smiling and laughing a bit more. It will increase your engagement level and make the whole experience a whole lot more fun for you and others!

Eye Contact

I want you to think about the power of eye contact. When we are nervous, we are more likely to look down or look away. Think about what happens when you are walking down a city street. You see someone coming towards you, your eyes meet, you are getting closer to each other, ready to pass by, and someone diverts eyes down or away. Hmmm. What would happen if you held the eye contact, smiled and said "hello"? You might make someone's day. You might stand up a bit taller. You might get a confidence boost. Your energy level just went up, my friend.

Let me remind you that people can see when you have wandering eyes. They notice when you look away from them and when you are scanning the room for "better opportunities." This may be unconscious on your part, but it sends a very clear signal to other people that they don't matter to you that much. When you are networking with someone, show that person respect by giving your full attention. Look that person in the eye, and be with him or her, even if just for a short time. This will help improve your connection and create the opportunity for a networking relationship to develop.

Handshakes

Nothing bugs me more than a weak, incomplete handshake. Whether from a man or a woman, I feel sad and disappointed when someone puts a limp fish hand in mine. Of course, there's the opposite problem – too much force, too much pressure. You are now hurting me physically. That doesn't help build rapport with me.

Learn to give a professional handshake. It should be complete, connecting you hand to hand; it should be equal, ensuring that both people's hands are in the vertical position, neither party dominating or submitting to the other. And it should be receptive and welcoming. Strive to apply the same level of pressure that you receive.

The difficult part about a handshake is that it happens so quickly. It's the usually the first and last thing you do with people. How do you know how much pressure to apply? I suggest that you read the other person's body language, and allow your kinesthetic sense to guide you. Don't assume that all women prefer a softer handshake. There are tennis players and other female athletes who have a very firm handshake. If you overdo it or underdo it, you can always ask to redo that handshake. "Let's try that again" can be a great thing to say if the first time didn't work so well.

Hugging and Kissing

I often get asked about whether it's appropriate to hug and kiss when greeting people. This one is hard because I am a very huggy type of person, but I have also learned the lesson that it is not always appropriate.

I was in Germany coordinating a European trade show on behalf of my company. I had been living in England for two years working with all our offices around Europe. It was pretty confusing for a young American to figure out the right number of kisses:

I was meeting two gentlemen from a German trade show company for the first time. One gentleman was quite large – at least three times my size. I suddenly questioned myself, not knowing what the proper greeting for this situation was. In a panic, I walked over to the German man, shook his hand and gave him a kiss on the right cheek and one on the left. I pulled back only to see him blush. I looked over at the other German man and could see him laugh and smile. He was ready for his. Cultural faux pas!

In the end, this was harmless, but it sure has stuck with me for many years. There are nuances from culture to culture and country to country that must be studied and understood in advance. How much touching? What kind of touch? How much personal space? Even eye contact rules are different. When in doubt, ask.

Alan Pease, author of *The Definitive Book of Body Language*, has this to say about international greeting norms:

> The Scandinavians are happy with a single kiss, the French most prefer a double, while the Dutch, Belgians, and Arabs go for a triple kiss. The Australians, New Zealanders, and Americans are continually confused about greeting kisses and bump noses as they fumble their way through a single peck. The Brits either avoid

kissing by standing back or will surprise you with a European double kiss.

Oh, and Japan – no touching, as bodily contact is considered impolite. Japanese people bow on first meeting with the holder of the highest status bowing the least and the one with the lowest status bowing the most.

And Germany? It's on the "don't touch" list, according to Dr. Ken Cooper, author of *Bodybusiness: The Sender's and Receiver's Guide to Nonverbal Communication*.

Do your research in advance, so that you can avoid any embarrassing situations. Or make it your policy that you don't hug or kiss on the first networking meeting. Get to know each other well before you get that close.

"Great people talk about ideas, average people talk about things, and small people talk about wine."
-Fran Lebowitz (1977)

9. GOING THE EXTRA MILE

Showing Up and Following Up are the Keys to Your Success

Have you ever been driving on the highway and worried that you missed the exit? Maybe you are not exactly sure where this destination is, but your gut tells you that you've already passed it. When this happens to me, I remind myself to stay the course. My destination is just around the bend. Call this persistence if you will, but it is spooky how often it turns out to be true. Turning around prematurely is counterproductive. You must have faith that the destination lies ahead. You must go that extra mile.

The same holds true in networking. Sometimes new connections you make don't immediately pan out. They do not appear to produce the great results that you had hoped for or were led to believe would happen by the person who connected you.. Now is the time to stay the course and not abandon this new relationship prematurely. It could help take you to great new places if you give the relationship the time to take you there.

How do you make this happen? First you show up, and then you practice systematic follow-up. Let me give you an example of how these two guiding principles of networking helped me create a powerful networking relationship that otherwise would not have been available to me. It's the story of how I met Juli Ann Reynolds, then CEO of the Tom Peters consulting company, and how I developed a professional networking relationship with her. This relationship continues to produce value in my life and business to this day.

Lesson No. 1: You Must Show Up,
Even if It Is Against All
Odds

Several years ago, I belonged to the MENG association, which stands for Marketing Executive Networking Group. My friend

Shirley had recommended that I join this group to help support my new business launch as a marketing consultant. One particular meeting was being held in Boston, which entailed a three-hour drive each way for me, and the meeting was at night. I had made arrangements to travel with my friend Shirley to the meeting, but she canceled on me at the very last minute. I remember being parked at the gas station making the decision to continue without her to the meeting. I'm not a very good night driver. I get sleepy, and I get lost a lot, especially in new areas. However, I was pretty motivated to go since Juli Ann Reynolds was the speaker and the group was discussing the power of personal branding. I was very interested in this topic, and I have been a long-time fan of business guru and author Tom Peters, founder of the Tom Peters Company.

On my way to Boston, I almost turned back three separate times. In fact, I was within one mile of the meeting but could not find the building within the Charlestown Naval Yard. I flagged down a police officer and even he did not know. So there I was so close but yet so lost. I overcame my fear and recommitted to showing up. I had come too far to turn back now. I parked the car and went door to door, asking strangers for directions until I found the building.

Did I mention that I was 90 minutes late to the meeting? And it was scheduled to be only a two-hour meeting. But I walked in, made my apologies for being tardy and quickly found a seat and began to participate in the very interesting discussion.

After the meeting, I made a point to introduce myself to Juli Ann, shake her hand and exchange business cards with her. I thanked her for hosting the MENG meeting at her swanky urban offices. It was a great evening all the way around.

Lesson No. 2: You Must Follow Up with People You Meet

A few days later, I rang Juli Ann and thanked her again. I told her what I had taken away from her talk and what I intended to do with the information. I then asked her if she would be willing to network with me from time to time. She accepted.

During a period of six months, we touched base a few times. She was very good at returning my phone calls. She even invited me up to the office to meet a few of her colleagues. They were looking for motivated marketing consultants to help them grow their training and consulting business. She even invited me to participate in a special train-the-trainer workshop for their Brand You! Program. I attended this two-day event and met more interesting people who have since become part of my professional network.

Several months later, she called me and asked if I would do a motivational talk for one of their clients who was having a sales meeting in Mystic, Connecticut. That was a paid speaking gig!

I brought her a prospective business opportunity that I was developing for a John Deere® dealership chain in the South. Interestingly, Juli Ann grew up on a farm in Nebraska, so she could relate to much of the John Deere® world. Unfortunately, the timing of our proposal coincided with the U.S. economic meltdown in 2008-2009, so the opportunity was put on hold.

Later that year, I had the opportunity to introduce Juli Ann to a client of mine who runs a national insurance company. Juli Ann and Diane reminded me of each other: They were both women, about the same age, both CEOs of companies; they had both broken through the glass ceiling and not only survived but also succeeded in male-dominated industries. They even looked alike. So naturally, I thought to connect them.

Within two weeks of my introduction, they had spoken on the telephone. They both are clearly motivated networkers and understand the power and importance of expanding your professional network. Even when you are at the top of your career game, you need a robust professional network to continue to build your success and opportunity.

When I think back on this story, it occurs to me that it would not have been possible if I didn't push through my own internal barriers and made the effort to show up. Staying at home or staying in the office day and night will not help you grow your professional network. There is a great deal of benefit to be had from getting out of the office regularly.

This story also illustrates the importance of follow-up. I wonder how many people at that MENG meeting actually reached out to Juli Ann after the meeting and set a course to develop a relationship with her. I might have been the only one to do so. This is why I recommend that you always make the effort to introduce yourself to the speaker. These are the kind of subject-matter experts that you want to add to your circle of influence. Think about this (and act upon it) the next time you go to a meeting, conference or convention.

Years in the Making

I've been curious about how staying in touch through time pans out to create networking and business success. The following personal story from my networking friend Chris Amorosino inspired me. Chris is a copywriter extraordinaire with an intriguing approach to business writing: "Writing Business Stories That Live Profitably Ever After." The same could be said about the magic of staying in touch with people in your network.

Networking fairy tales do come true. Here's one such example from Chris:

> Years ago I was a lowly newsletter writer at a trade association when a senior vice president walked into my tiny cubicle. This SVP was someone everyone in my department admired. We thought he'd end up being president of the association one day. He had never been in my cubicle before, and since I was not part of his division, his visit was curious.

The SVP began quizzing me about book publishing. After 10 minutes or so, I stopped him and tried to ask politely why he was asking me all these questions. He told me that he planned to write a book one day and was doing some fact gathering.

I never forgot that. If this intelligent, talented senior executive was writing a book and was asking me for information, I planned to stay in touch. About a year later, the SVP left the association. I would call him every six months or so to ask if he was ready to start on his book. He never was.

A few years later, I left the association. Still, I kept in touch with the former SVP. Now in the age of e-mail, I would shoot him a message every so often to ask about the book inside his head. More than eight years after our first conversation, the SVP contacted me to say he was ready to write his book. It took three-and-a-half years after that day to write and publish the 20-chapter book. But what a great project!

I got to work with a very smart person. He allowed me to add some enhancements to his book, including eight cartoons and one chapter. When the book arrived from the press, I felt as close as a man can feel to giving birth. What a great feeling!

Perhaps this isn't a pure networking story, but it does speak to one basic of networking: staying in touch. You never know when a prospect or client is going to need you. You always want to be top of mind. I earned a nice paycheck on that project and received follow-up work. But better yet was the thrill of helping someone spread the wealth of his knowledge to a wide audience. As I write this, I can look three feet to my left and see that book sitting on my shelf. Life is good.

Chris's networking success took 11 years to incubate before it manifested into business success. Do you have that kind of patience and faith? Would you like to?

Consistency Pays Off

Woody Allen got it mostly right in his famous quote, "Eighty percent of success is showing up." I like to think that follow-up is the remaining twenty percent of the success quotient. Absenteeism, whether literal or figurative, doesn't do much for your visibility and connection to the community. While showing up is critical in networking and relationship-building, you must go the extra mile with timely and consistent follow-up. There are serious goodies and rewards to be gained through networking as long as you practice patience and disciplined follow-up. I like to think that those who show up, go up and those who follow up, go up in growth.

"The world is run by those who show up."
-Robert B. Johnson and Richard G. Weingardt writing in the
Journal of Management in Engineering, Jan/Feb 1999

10. Drive an Automatic

How to Systematize Your Networking Follow-Up

There's a reason that the majority of new cars are built and sold with automatic transmissions. It makes driving a car easier. You have to perform fewer steps in order to commandeer the vehicle. Of course, some manual transmission buffs don't believe that this is real driving (and that repair costs can actually be higher). But I hope you'll agree with me that the fewer steps you have to remember, the easier the process is.

When it comes to networking, the task of follow-up can overwhelm people and create actual stress in their lives. They are bombarded with business cards that they don't know what to do with, phone calls and e-mails they don't have time to make or answer. They are already overbooked with their job and family responsibilities. Who has time to stay in touch?

I have a solution for this classic dilemma. You need to create an organized, systematic method of networking follow-up. I suggest that you employ the THERAPY model of motivated networking follow-up. Here's what's involved:

> **T = Targeted:** You must put some targeting strategy into your networking game plan.

> **H = Helpful:** Find simple, creative and time-efficient ways to be more helpful to the people in your professional network.

> **E = Efficient:** Whatever system you plan to use, it must be highly efficient; otherwise you won't do it consistently.

> **R = Reliable:** You must strive to be highly reliable with your networking follow-up. You must fulfill the promises that you make in a timely and consistent manner.

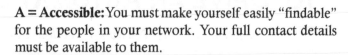

A = Accessible: You must make yourself easily "findable" for the people in your network. Your full contact details must be available to them.

P = Personalized: To break through the clutter, your networking follow-up must be personalized. It must feel like it could only be from you and only for them.

Y = Yippee, Yahoo!: You should have fun with your follow-up. It can be something that brings joy and creates energy in your life and others' lives as well.

Let's break down each one of these factors and figure out how to incorporate it into your networking follow-up system. This will allow you to drive your professional network more easily and more effectively.

Targeting Your Network Strategy

In Chapter 3, "What Road to Take," we discussed the importance of identifying who in your network was most important to you. Who can help you get the farthest fastest? Which relationships are most critical to your life, career and business? This is where you need to spend the majority of your networking time and energy. These people are the pistons in the engine of your professional network. They help you keep things cranking along.

To take care of these important relationships, your follow-up needs to be more frequent and special. These people matter to you. Don't ignore them or take them for granted. Check in with them every five weeks or so. Offer to help them in any way you can. Introduce them to people that they want to meet. Cultivate and develop these top relationships over time. Spend quality face time with them.

The other aspect about targeting is knowing who doesn't add value to your network. Yes, know who your "duds" are, and limit the amount of time and energy you devote to them. You can do this gently and even indirectly, but limit the time you spend with them. Here's where no follow-up is a good strategy. You have decided not to encourage this relationship, not to develop it further. This is a perfectly OK thing to do. It fact, it is often a smart decision. Don't invest your time and energy in people and relationships that bring you down or pull you back. These people (they may be in your immediate family or close circles) can be poisonous to your professional and personal development.

Now that you are more targeted with your networking strategy, we can move on to how you can use your time and energy more creatively to be helpful (and valuable) to the people in your professional network.

Being Helpful is Easier than You Think

Networking is about building and maintaining mutually beneficial relationships before you need them. So how do you add more benefit to your networking? How can you be more helpful to other people without making it a demanding full-time, Good Samaritan extra job?

My first idea for you is to stop sending all of those e-mails. Swear off the "reply all" button. Many busy professionals that I know get more than 100 e-mails a day. They are overwhelmed by the sheer sight of their e-mail inbox. Your well-intended e-mail networking follow-up is not a gift; it feels more like a burden. You need to give more thought to the other person and how that person likes to be communicated with, not just what's convenient for you.

Here are some creative ideas on how you can be more helpful to the people in your professional network:

1. Connect them with someone in your network who you think can help them.

2. Write a recommendation on LinkedIn®.

3. Leave them short, clear and concise voice mails, and

remember to include your telephone number (say it slowly twice).

4. Send them articles that you read and think might be of interest to them.

5. When the postal rates go up, send them the 1-cent or 2-cent stamps that make up the difference, saving them a trip to the post office.

6. Send them a gift certificate to Dunkin' Donuts or Starbucks with a short message, "Enjoy a coffee on me."

7. Alert them if you find a typo in their materials or in their online profile. Of course, do this gently and without judgment. You want them to look good.

8. Send them a copy of your favorite professional development book, DVD or audio training CD (or how about this one?).

9. Keep them motivated by sending messages of support and encouragement.

10. Congratulate and acknowledge their accomplishments.

11. Alert them to any news or information about their company or industry. You want them to be "in the know."

12. If you have a Web site or blog, offer them the opportunity to contribute a guest article. Feature their expertise with your visitors and fans.

13. Alert them of interesting upcoming events. Invite them to join you. You don't have to pay their way; you just want them to have the same opportunity that you have.

14. Share your lessons learned with them.

15. Help them think through a current challenge.

16. Offer them candid and constructive feedback. (Note: first, secure their permission. Unsolicited feedback can

sometimes backfire. Start by asking the question "Are you open to some feedback?" or "Would you like some feedback on that?")

17. Let them know if you see an interesting job opening that they or someone in their network may want to know about.

18. Share best practices and coach each other.

19. Offer to play the role of their accountability partner. Find out what their major goal is, what is keeping them from accomplishing it and offer to hold them accountable to a specific deadline. Structure this arrangement so it works for both of you.

20. Help them understand their personal brand. Tell them what you admire most about them and how they are uniquely different from other people.

Efficiency Is Essential for Your Follow-Up Success

I believe that disorganization will kill you, and it will be a slow, painful death. You can avoid that by putting some organization, discipline and efficiency into how you approach your networking follow-up. The good news is that even if this is not part of your DNA, you can hire outside professional organizers to help you improve in this area.

When it comes to increasing the efficiency of your networking follow-up system, you need to have a Web-based contact management system to organize and update the many connections you will make through your networking. I recommend having one online system so you can access it 24/7 from anywhere in the world. The old Rolodex™ system, with the spinning racks that held the business cards, was a terrific solution in its day, but now we have more advanced technology to help us take our organization to the next level of efficiency and access. Excel spreadsheets are good, but there are better systems out there that you should be investigating.

Shop around, and ask other people you know what contact management system they use and what they like and dislike about it. You might consider a CRM (customer relationship management) system. While these systems typically are designed to support the sales process, they may offer you some additional functionality that could boost your productivity and efficiency when it comes to networking follow-up.

It's important to note that you need to collect more contact information on the people you meet in networking. E-mail addresses are not enough. You want to record telephone (and cell phone) numbers, full mailing addresses and even birthdays and personal information. This becomes important and relevant as you build a closer relationship with them through time. The contact management system you select must accommodate your future needs as well as your immediate ones.

So where do you have your contact information now? Is it scattered all over your desk? Do you have bundles of business cards held together by rubber bands, tucked away in your office? Do you have some of the contacts on your e-mail account, some on your cell phone and some stashed away other places? It's time to consolidate all this information. If you are feeling overwhelmed and don't know where to start, the first thing you need to do is to hire an assistant. Interview a few of them. And, yes, pay that person out of your own pocket. Your current disorganization is costing you more than you know. You can pay someone to help you resolve this problem. It's time to get organized and more efficient with the people in your professional network.

How Reliable Are You?

The golden rule in networking is: If you offer to help someone, you must fulfill that promise promptly and completely. If you don't, your professional reputation may be at risk. You don't want to be known as a ball-dropper or someone who talks a good game, but doesn't come through in the end.

I know that most of us don't set out to be unreliable; it often happens because life is very demanding and everyone wants a piece of our time and attention. Our intention is to help others, and sometimes in our enthusiasm, we make promises that are realistically very difficult to fulfill. But the problem still remains. Overpromising and under-delivering in any context are damaging to your reputation.

Here's one possible solution: If during the course of networking with someone, you can think of multiple connections for that person, ask which one of these introductions would be most useful right now. Force that person to make a choice. If he or she says all of them, gently suggest picking one connection to start. After completing this connection, the individual can contact you to get the next introduction. This method helps focus all parties and reduces the possibility of anyone being overwhelmed and the risk of inaction. Even job-seekers can get overwhelmed with a list of three to five people they need to contact following your meeting.

The final suggestion I have to help you improve your reliability in networking is to make it a greater priority. Every time you follow up on a promise or offer that you have made to someone else, you are putting pennies into the equity bank of your professional reputation. These small investments compound and multiply over time. Your relationship and your results from networking will also be elevated.

Make Yourself Easily Accessible

Unless you are in the witness protection program, you will want to be found by other people, old friends and new friends alike. I realize that some people are more private in nature and don't like to promote themselves out there with big personalities. Even in these cases, you can help the people in your close personal circles get in touch and stay in touch with you more easily by keeping your contact information updated and easily available to them. Don't make them go hunting for your contact details. Don't leave voice mails without leaving your name and telephone number. Don't send e-mails without a signature that has contact information below it.

Why? Because I might just want to get in touch with you, but the thought of searching for your contact information might be enough to let this opportunity pass me by. By making yourself more easily "findable," you increase the chances of people returning your phone calls, responding to you and staying in touch with you.

If you leave one job and start another, please let me know about that. Send me your new contact details. Don't allow yourself to go missing off my radar screen. Help me keep track of you and all the exciting (or not so exciting) changes in your life.

How can you be more accessible online? Open an account on LinkedIn® and Facebook®. For you more advanced social media mavens, get a Twitter™ account. Put these Web site addresses in your e-mail signature, so they are automatically posted every time you send me an e-mail. Put a photo that I recognize (current and professional) on your profile page. I went to search for my uncle Carlos Garcia on LinkedIn®. Thankfully, he had a professional photo portrait on his profile; otherwise it would have been difficult for me to find him. Do you know how many Carlos Garcias there are in America? Please don't put your baby picture, photos of your kids or your horse on your profile. I won't recognize you as easily. Your efforts to be cute create difficulty and sometimes mistrust for me. Put your real face with your real name. Now I can find you.

How can you be more accessible offline? When using the traditional communication channels, such as telephone and "snail mail," remember to put your return address and return telephone number. Think about your voice mail recorded greeting. In fact, call yourself now, and listen to it. Is it professional? Does it provide all the information that I need to get hold of you? Do you have energy in your voice that will motivate me to leave a message and get in touch with you? Or do you sound like the living dead?

How can you be more accessible for face-to-face interaction? Make time for me. Feed me. As author Keith Ferrazzi says in his fabulous, highly recommended book on networking, you should *Never Eat Alone*. Make connections with people when you are refueling yourself by sharing lunch, meeting for breakfast or having dinner with people in your network. While I appreciate that this can be very time consuming, plus expensive, relationships are enhanced with quality face time. If food is an issue, then meet for a walk and get exercise together. If golf is a passion, then meet at the driving range after work, and shoot a bucket of balls together or play nine holes. Meet for a manicure or pedicure. Whatever it is that you enjoy and allows you to spend quality time with people whom you care about, make time to do it together.

The last idea I have for you about making yourself accessible in face-to-face situations is rideshare together. Don't drive alone to conferences and meetings. Rather, arrange to drive together. You will have concentrated time to chat and catch up and get to where you need to be – together! Not only will you save gas and lighten up your carbon footprint, you will enhance your networking relationships.

Get Personal with Your Networking Follow-Up

Whether you have a formal or informal style, you can develop closer relationships with your networking contacts by sharing more of yourself with them. Every time you follow up, I want you to ask yourself whether you are truly expressing your personal brand and honoring theirs, or are you communicating in the expected, standard, "professional way." Some of you may not agree with me on this next point, but if your networking follow-up reads more like a cover letter for a job interview, then you are missing the personal touch.

Getting personal in your follow-up to me looks like this:

1. Send your contacts a birthday card on their birthdays. Better yet, call and sing them "Happy Birthday" on their special day. No matter how bad you think your voice is, the singing telegram is a powerful gift you can give.

2. Send personalized greeting cards, either handwritten or typed using your personal handwriting font. SendOutCards® is what I use. Check it out at my Web site MotivatingCards.com.

3. Send a photo of the two of you, which you took during your last meeting. When the person opens your card, e-mail or letter, he or she instantly smiles seeing a visual memory of a good experience.

4. Your follow-up contains reference to specific information that you discussed. It's not generic in any way.

5. You use personalized salutations such as "Dear Kathy" and signature closures. I like to use the word "Cheers" above my signature line. I picked up affection for this word while living and working in England for three years.

6. The voice mail message that you leave has an uplifting vocal quality. Just hearing your voice brings a smile to the person's face.

7. Use the person's name several times when leaving your voice mail messages. Everyone likes to hear the sound of his or her own name. Write the person's name a few times in your e-mail correspondence.

8. Personalize any invitation that you send through LinkedIn®. If you only use the standard LinkedIn® message header: "Because you are someone that I trust, I'd like to invite you to become part of my professional network," you will be saying "I was too lazy to write a personal message to you."

9. Write your LinkedIn® profile summary with a more personalized, conversational tone. Mine starts out, "Thank you for visiting my LinkedIn® page to learn more about me. I look forward to connecting with you and getting to know you. I work with_____ " (now I get to the meat of my experience, credentials and business focus).

Yippee! Who Says You Can't Have Fun with Your Follow-Up?

If something is a drag, you are not going to do it, at least not without putting up a fight or doing a lot of complaining about it. Whether that something is house cleaning, exercising or networking follow-up (three things you have to do, by the way), if you don't enjoy it, you won't make time for it, nor will you do it with much gusto.

How do you change something from painful to pleasurable? How do you alter your attitude, so that you enjoy something more than you did in the past?

Part of the solution is that with practice, you get good at it, and, as a result, your confidence and motivation will increase toward it. This reminds me of an excellent quote on the subject of motivation from the renowned author, speaker and leadership guru John C. Maxwell:

> The whole idea of motivation is a trap. Forget motivation. Just do it. Exercise, lose weight, test your blood sugar, or whatever. Do it without motivation. And then, guess what? After you start doing the thing, that's when the motivation comes and makes it easy for you to keep on doing it.

For me, people are fun. Relationships, while sometimes complex and confusing, are rewarding. Why not put a little more fun into how you interact with people in your professional network? Why not laugh a little bit more? Don't take yourself so seriously. Even a job search can be fun if you set your mind to it.

You can approach networking like a game or an experiment. Take a few risks, and measure the results. Read some more books on the subject. Try your hand at a speed networking exercise.

This may be easy for me to say because I have made this my focus, my passion, my expertise. But it wasn't always that way. I had to learn the ropes of networking by doing it and making mistakes along the way. I have been chewed out by a few people who didn't like my approach. It stung at the time, but I moved on. I didn't let them squelch my joy or my results from the very important professional skill of relationship-building.

Fun is a state of mind. You control that; no one else does. The good news is that you can instantly alter your state from moment to moment by thinking different thoughts, conjuring up great memories or making changes to your physiology (i.e., put a smile on your face, laugh, get up and move around). And, of course, the ultimate in fun is hanging around motivated, positive people who are passionate about what they do and can do in the world.

"Whoever said 'the fortune is in the follow-up' first, could have been a billionaire if they only got a penny for every time someone said it. And yet, they've only got it half right. Follow-up is important, that's true. But the real fortune is in the follow-up system."
-Lisa Robbin Young, "The Renaissance Mom"

11. ROADSIDE ASSISTANCE

Why You Should Join Your Local Chamber of Commerce or Other Networking Organizations

If you've ever been stranded on the road because of a flat tire, a mechanical breakdown or the embarrassing, "I can't believe this happened again, but I locked keys in the car," you're sure to be grateful for your AAA membership. One phone call and someone comes to rescue you. That's the beauty of roadside assistance – a must-have contingency plan for any driver.

But imagine you didn't have that resource, and you truly were stranded with no one to help you. You might be waiting (or walking) for quite a long time to solve the problem.

For small business owners, that roadside assistance is your local chamber of commerce. Big or small, your local chamber is an additional resource on your business team. It will advocate on your behalf with local and state government, it will provide programs to help sharpen your business acumen, it will help to promote your business and it will give you networking opportunities with other businesses owners, big and small.

The chamber of commerce system in the United States started in 1911 when President William H. Taft set into motion discussions that would launch the U.S. Chamber of Commerce, the world's largest business federation, with more than 3 million businesses across all 50 states. The main purpose of the chamber of commerce system is to promote and defend free enterprise and individual opportunity. With small businesses representing more than three-quarters of all new jobs in the United States, this sector has economic significance. Yet on their own without support, small businesses struggle to have their voices heard and to gain access to larger market opportunities as the big boys have. Let's face it; budgets are smaller.

But through this channel where enterprising people come together for advocacy, action and support, their collective voices can be heard. Together, they have greater influence on the economy than they would otherwise have operating alone.

I belong to two chambers of commerce, but have visited with many more in my role as a professional speaker and program provider. What I enjoy most about chambers of commerce is the accessibility to the executive directors and the relationships that you can build with these highly connected leaders. In fact, that is the main job of chambers of commerce – to connect people with opportunity and support the sustained growth of their members.

I have also done my share of griping and complaining that I didn't get much out of my local chamber membership. I ask myself: Why should I send them my money if I don't get the value? Of course, that situation is directly linked to my activity or lack of direct involvement with the chamber. Simply paying your chamber membership is a nice show of local support, but it's not enough to ensure you get personal value from your membership. You must get involved.

Here are 10 ways in which you can get more mileage from your chamber of commerce membership:

1. Personally get to know the executive director of your local chamber of commerce. Have coffee or lunch with him or her. Exchange business cards. Ask how you can be of service to the organization, in addition to how it can specifically support you.

2. Satisfy your professional development needs with the chamber's events and programming. Look at their calendar of events, and sign up for seminars, workshops and discussion groups. You will not only gain new knowledge and sharpen your business skills, but you will also meet and mingle with new people.

3. Select an industry forum or discussion group and attend their regular meetings and/or read their meeting notes.

Find out what's going down on the legislative front and how you can work to make positive changes through your chamber. This will help keep you up to speed on industry issues that could affect your business. It could even help to mitigate business taxes. Those who care, take action. Those that don't, just complain.

4. Contribute something of value to the chamber. For example, write an article for the newsletter or Web sites; host a networking event at your place of business; offer yourself or a member of your team as speaker or workshop leader. This platform will naturally spotlight your expertise and your company's capabilities, but you are also adding to the collective value to the chamber organization.

5. Don't just attend the events, but reach out to your fellow chamber members. Go through the membership roster and identify five to 10 companies and individuals that you'd like to get to know better. Call them and invite them to network with you over coffee. You already have something in common – your chamber membership. This personal outreach effort goes a long way to extending the value of your chamber membership. Don't just show up, but go out of your way to make connections and build relationships with your fellow chamber members.

6. If you make a good connection at a chamber event, remember to follow up and continue the conversation. Don't just collect business cards, but build relationships from within your chamber.

7. Invite others in your network to join your chamber of commerce. Become a friendly recruiter. Your executive director will love you for this, and you will be helping to keep the membership vibrant and interesting. Be sure to make a special effort to introduce your friend/guest to as many chamber members as you know. Help with their orientation whenever you can.

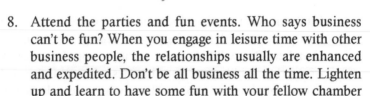

8. Attend the parties and fun events. Who says business can't be fun? When you engage in leisure time with other business people, the relationships usually are enhanced and expedited. Don't be all business all the time. Lighten up and learn to have some fun with your fellow chamber members.

9. Create link love with your chamber of commerce. List your chamber membership on your LinkedIn® account and on your company's Web site, if appropriate. Show your affiliation and commitment to building a strong local economy. Make sure your business listing is current and that your business is appropriately described on the chamber's Web site. Send your chamber of commerce copies of any press releases that you issue or for events that you are holding. It can help to co-promote you and your business. Why wouldn't you take advantage of these marketing resources? It's part of your membership!

10. Get the group discount. If reducing expenses is attractive to you, then you need to learn to leverage your chamber membership and affiliation to get discounts off products and services that you buy locally. Check out the member-to-member discounts offered by your chamber, and remember to inquire if chamber member discounts are available when you purchase things locally. The savings you make simply by inquiring could pay for your entire year chamber membership. I just reviewed the list of available member-to-member discounts that are available through my chamber, and I'm hitting myself now knowing all the money that I've left on the table. From coffee to printing to dry cleaning, I could have saved some money. It pays to ask for the member discount.

Don't go it alone. Accelerate your professional and business success by joining your local chamber of commerce and getting involved.

"Membership has its privileges."
-American Express advertising campaign

CHECKLIST #2

Good job! You've completed Part II of your networking journey. Part III will introduce you to strategies and tactics to help you accelerate your business networking success. When you have completed these actions, you will be ready for Part III.

☐ I am more consciously aware my body language and use of my voice and its importance in the networking and communication process.

☐ I have reflected upon my own personal brand and how I want to develop it.

☐ I have developed and practiced my 30-second elevator pitch and am more confident in introducing myself in networking situations.

☐ I have set up a contact management system that stores and organizes all of my networking contacts' information (including email, telephone, mailing address and personal data). It is easily accessible and I can add and update information to it with minimal effort.

☐ I have developed a personalized networking follow-up system that allows me to stay in touch more regularly with my networking contacts.

☐ I have joined and become active in one or more networking groups (e.g., Chamber of Commerce) and am committed to getting involved with its people and projects in order to maximize my benefits.

PART III

ACCELERATE YOUR SUCCESS
OVERCOME OBSTACLES
AND SPECIAL SITUATIONS

12. Autobahn Ahead

Networking for Business Acceleration

I remember the very first time that I was in Germany and experienced driving on an autobahn. I was the passenger of my German colleague who was driving a gorgeous black Mercedes Benz with cool leather interior. When we merged onto the autobahn and he put his foot on the accelerator, that car just took off. I found myself bracing and going completely silent. My eyes stared at the speedometer as it climbed to 150 kilometers per hour. What was even more startling was when he decelerated to comply with the posted signs once the autobahn stretch had ended. It was like going on a rollercoaster, only not knowing that you were in line to ride.

I later learned that the autobahn, or Bundesautobahn (BAB) as it is officially called, is the federal motorway system that was built in Germany in the 1920s. Switzerland and Austria also have an autobahn system as part of their roadways. The autobahn has no general speed limits. While officials post an advisory speed limit (usually around 130 kilometers per hour or 81 miles per hour), you can go as fast as you feel is safe. Seat belts are required for everyone in the vehicle. There are no speeding tickets or fines for driving too fast on the autobahn; the only risk you take is increasing your insurance liability in the event of an accident.

The Need for Speed

There are times in your life when you need to pick up the speed and get bigger things done. This is particularly relevant in business development. There are professionals who specialize in this discipline and are highly compensated and sought after for their ability to "make rain" and grow the company. Their ability to attract new customers and penetrate new markets makes them highly valuable to any organization. Yet, this skill set can and should be developed by anyone who wants to grow professional success.

"I want to be a finder, not a grinder." This statement was made by my friend and client Carol, who is a partner at a successful mid-sized law firm in Connecticut. Carol had realized long ago that in order to move up the ranks and increase her compensation, it wasn't enough just to do excellent work and put in long hours. She had to bring in work to the firm. She had to learn how to "make rain" by increasing her competence and confidence in networking and business development. Carol also realized that she needed to teach the other women at the firm how to do the same.

No matter what your field of expertise – law, accounting, technology, business – your value to the organization will be enhanced if you can master the basics of business development, which include forming strategic relationships.

Get in the Fast Lane with Strategic Moves

When business development is the goal, your networking strategy needs to be finely tuned. You cannot rely on serendipity or take a casual relaxed approach to building your professional network. You need to make strategic moves and build strategic relationships that can take you somewhere significant soon. You must develop an appetite for greater risk and actively push yourself out of your comfort zone. It's time to be bolder and connect to people of greater influence. You have a business to build.

Adopt the Attitude and Behavior of the Rainmaker

The modern definition of a rainmaker is an employee of a company who creates a large amount of unexpected business, consistently brings in money at critical times or brings in markedly more money than his or her co-workers, thereby "floating their salaries." Every organization needs a few rainmakers on the team.

Personally, I don't think you are born a rainmaker, but rather you can learn the skills and disposition to become one. Following the fundamentals of business development activity, let's take a look at what that might mean in terms of networking:

1. Assess market opportunity: In networking terms, you need to understand specifically who can potentially help you advance your business. Who might need what you have to offer? Start by thinking about the types of businesses, occupations and individuals who may benefit from partnering with you on your venture. Drill down into narrower chunks, identifying specific segments within the larger sphere that you think may show greater interest in your value proposition. Write all of this down.

2. Gather intelligence: Do your research. Get yourself to your local library and ask the business librarian to show you how to access the numerous databases (one of the free benefits of being a card-carrying member of your local library). In addition to the information you can find online, in directories and in books, research and read articles written by or about your target. Talk to other people in your network who know your potential targets, personally or professionally. Find out where they hang out, and what associations they belong to. Create profiles of the companies and individuals that you identified in step one. Start to prioritize them according to their potential opportunity for you. Once again, write all of this down.

3. Generate leads: Once you have done your homework it's time to reach out and connect with people who are directly and indirectly related to your target. Your goal is to get as close to target as quickly as possible. Rather than targeting the long and winding road, find the shortest distances to your success path. Who knows someone who can introduce you to your target? Each one of these

new connections along the way also becomes a valuable addition to your professional network. Be open and responsive to the other ideas and connections that they may offer you. Keep your peripheral vision active.

4. Follow up on activity: Rainmakers are masters at follow-up. They are organized and disciplined and have a process and system for staying in regular touch. There's no sense in generating leads if you are going to let them languish with poor follow-up. Think about each lead as potentially being worth a million dollars to you. Handle them with extreme care and attention.

5. Know your value proposition and rehearse your pitch: When you get serious about business development, you will find that "winging it" is not in your best interest. You've worked too hard to get this far. It's worth your time and effort to practice your pitch and rehearse your presentations. You must be able to articulate your compelling proposition in a few short minutes. Knowing what you want to communicate and being confident about your ability to deliver it effectively will increase your chances of moving to the next step on your business development timeline. Practice makes perfect; rehearsal primes rain.

6. Present yourself and your opportunity to others: Now that you've rehearsed, it's time to get this show on the road. Think about the phrase "location, location, location." You need to be where others gather; know where they go, so that you can meet each other and get to know each other in the networking environment. This is an excellent primer to the future business dealings. If you can make your first encounter outside the normal business office environment, you stand a greater chance to getting an invitation in the door. Cold calls are just that – cold. Networking

introductions and meeting people in the networking context is a great warm-up to discussing new business opportunities with them.

7. Design your business model: You have to be very clear about how you plan to make money. Who can afford your products and services and who can't or won't? Networking for business development demands that you "follow the money." If this expression turns you off, think about the value of your time. Do you want to waste it, or do you want to make the most of it? Being very clear on your "who strategy" will help accelerate your networking and business success. When you are rich, your reward can be networking just for the fun of it. Until then, practice strategic networking for business development.

8. Planning and monitoring performance: Just like anything you do in business, you must set measurable networking goals and track progress against them. "What gets measured, gets done," my old boss used to say to me. Don't allow yourself to fly by the seat of the pants when it comes to networking. Chart it, graph it, show percent to goal – whatever you need to do to report to yourself how you are doing. If you need help, get an accountability partner, and have that person call you every week and ask you to report on your progress. There's something about having to confess failure to someone else that motivates people to regular action and progress.

9. Campaign development. As your network grows and you make important new leads and connections, you will want a campaign to stay in regular touch with them. According to Jeffrey Forman, publisher of The Renegade Network Marketer Review, "For every month that we don't contact or communicate with our client, we lose 10% of our influence." Mr. Forman lists this on his "scary

business facts" page. If this finding is true, I imagine that it wouldn't take long to deplete all that you've worked so hard to build. Your business development success strategy must include a plan to touch base with these important people at least once per quarter. Four times a year will help you stay visible and relevant to them. When opportunity knocks, you want to be near the door to open it.

"Speed matters."
-Eric Morham, president, Vincor Canada

13. NEVER DRIVE A COLD CAR

Warm Up Your Networking Introductions

Cold is not comfortable. Living in the northeastern part of the United States, I know it can be pretty miserable to get into your car after a cold, snowy night. The windshield is iced over, the seats are cold and the engine is not happy. Modern advances such as garages, heated seats and automatic starters have taken the edge off this problem, but the memory of it reminds me of a problem that most professionals have when it comes to networking and meeting new people: They drive cold.

You've got to warm things up and get more specific about who you want to meet. This is part of a strategy that I call "Aim Higher. Get Warmer."

Know What You Want and Where You Want to Go

The first part of this strategy involves the power of specificity. You wouldn't walk into a fancy restaurant and say, "Please give me some food," and expect a fabulous meal that was exactly what you wanted. You may be really hungry, but it helps when you can narrow down the category of what would be appealing to you. This not only helps the wait staff, but helps you get a better, more satisfying outcome.

One of the wonderful outcomes of networking is that when you build a relationship with others, they are more open to introducing you to people they know. You can help them to help you by being specific in terms of whom you are looking to meet. If they don't know this person, they just might know someone who does. The theory of six degrees of separation suggests that you are within six connections from any person on Earth. That's an amazing, almost unbelievable, concept. Here's an intriguing excerpt from the play Six Degrees of Separation written by John

Guare in 1990, which was later made into a movie featuring actors Donald Sutherland and Mary Beth Hurt:

> I read somewhere that everybody on this planet is separated by only six other people. Six degrees of separation. Between us and everybody else on this planet. The president of the United States. A gondolier in Venice. Fill in the names. I find that a) tremendously comforting that we're so close; and b) like Chinese water torture that we're so close. Because you have to find the right six people to make the connection. It's not just big names. It's anyone. A native in a rain forest. A Tierra del Fuegan. An Eskimo. I am bound to everyone on this planet by a trail of six people. It's a profound thought.... How every person is a new door, opening up into other worlds. Six degrees of separation between me and everyone else on this planet. But to find the right six people.

> - Monologue by Ouisa Kitteredge, a character in the 1990 play *Six Degrees of Separation* written by John Guare

To tap into this idea, you must be able to articulate whom you are looking to meet. Whom in your "future network" have you identified that you'd like to meet and potentially build a relationship with? Be more targeted in your thinking, do your research and name a living human being who interests you. Know generally why you are motivated to meet that person. Then find a way through your network of being introduced to that person. Ask for a "warm introduction." A warm introduction is when someone introduces you versus making a cold call yourself. A warm introduction will be far easier and more effective than cold-calling or conducting some passive or aggressive marketing campaign. In my book, people always make the best conduits to other people.

A Networking Experiment

A few years ago I was coaching a corporate "rising star" – someone identified by his organization as high potential talent with leadership aspirations. As part of my executive coaching program, I was teaching him how to network more effectively and build relationships inside and outside the organization. Most corporate professionals I know (and I was one for 22 years!) are usually so buried in their projects that they rarely look up or look around.

When I asked this gentleman who was in his active network, he named about five people he was working closely with in his company. When I asked him who he'd like to add to his future network, he was quiet. He gave me that deer-in-the-headlights look. He couldn't answer the question. He hadn't thought about it – ever. When I pushed him further, he blurted out the name of the CEO of a large Fortune 500 technology company. He was aiming high. I respected that. We discussed how we might make that happen for him, but I'm not sure he was really serious about this goal. He just wanted me off his back for now.

As I was driving home from the coaching session, I reached out and called my friend and former colleague Shirley, who now lives in Southern California. She and I had stayed in touch since we both left a leading direct mail company a few years back. We were both motivated to keep our relationship alive and stay in each other's active network. A call every three months or so seemed to be the glue that our relationship needed to survive the 3,000-mile distance between us.

I casually shared this experience with Shirley, and she surprised me with, "Kathy, you'll never guess who I got e-mail from yesterday. Our ex-colleague was just appointed to a top executive position at that very company." This intrigued me, but the gentleman who she named was not familiar to me. I had left the company just before he joined. But Shirley had worked closely with him and respected him greatly. I smiled, took a deep breath and popped the question to Shirley.

"Shirley, do you want to participate in a little networking experiment that I am conducting?" I asked in a playful tone of voice. "What do you have in mind?" she asked. "If you will introduce me to this gentleman, then I will ask him if he will meet with my client, who, by the way, is traveling out to attend the company's convention in three weeks. Perhaps they could meet for coffee. Are you game?" I asked her. "Game on," she replied.

Within 24 hours, I received an e-mail from Shirley informing me that she had connected with this gentleman, and he had agreed to do it. "Ball's in your court," her e-mail informed me.

Now the moment of truth. I had to make a call to a person I didn't know. Not just any person, but a Fortune 500 top executive. I stood up to make the call (a physiology that I find gives me more courage and gumption) and dialed his home number. It was Friday afternoon, and it was now or never. I needed to take the next step in this experiment – for my client's sake and for the lesson.

He answered the phone. I quickly introduced myself and referenced Shirley's referral. I told him about my client and what I was teaching him. I asked him if he would meet my client for coffee when he was at the convention in San Francisco in a few weeks time. He agreed, but on one condition. I listened eagerly. This savvy business leader asked if my client would come prepared to answer a few questions: Why did his company choose them as a vendor? What about times when they chose not to work with them and why not? What other competitors do they use and why? It turns out that my client's organization is a customer of this Fortune 500 business. This "voice of the customer" was an interesting way to get oriented to a new industry and new job. I agreed to these terms on behalf of my client. The experiment had moved to the next stage.

Three weeks later, my client and this top leader met for coffee in San Francisco. It was a good exchange, and my client certainly appreciated the connection and opportunity. I encouraged him to follow up to continue to foster the relationship. Ironically, my client's boss told me later on that he personally knew the CEO of that Fortune 500 company. As it turns out, my client was only one degree of separation away from his target contact. Funny how that works.

Now's here where the networking magic worked for me. As I reached out to this top executive to thank him for meeting with my client, I asked him if there was anything that I could do for him in return. He e-mailed back to say that he could use some help finding temporary housing in the Palo Alto area and that his wife was looking to join a golf club. Did I know of any good ones in the area? Ironically, this is where I grew up and went to college. And while it had been a while since I lived in the area, I still had strong connections to people who could possibly help with this request.

I immediately jumped into action and accessed my network – both professional and personal. Guess who turned out to be the most useful contact for me? My mother. She forwarded my request to my old neighbors, with whom I had lost touch, and friends of the family. Within 36 hours, I had several local area experts giving me "the insider's scoop" on the best places to live and to play golf in the area. I felt empowered to be able to go back to my new networking contact with some specific information and ideas that might help him get settled more easily.

I also reached out via LinkedIn® and sent this gentleman an invitation. He accepted it. I read his online profile in depth and looked at the other connections he had listed on LinkedIn®. This gentleman had once again proved to me that he was a motivated networker. His behavior, willingness and online profile demonstrated that he knew how to network and knew the power and importance of relationships.

I like to think that this networking experiment was a success on several fronts. I also consider it an ongoing experiment. Time will tell the value of this new connection.

> *"The way of the world is meeting people through other people."*
> -Robert Kerrigan (finestquotes.com)

members in more than 200 countries (as of August 2010). A new member joins LinkedIn® approximately every second, and about half its members are outside the United States. Executives from all Fortune 500 companies are LinkedIn® members.

Everybody's Doing It

This number pales in comparison to Facebook® and Twitter™. DigitalBuzzBlog.com posted data compiled by Website-Monitoring.com on the leading social media networking sites.

According to the report as of March 16, 2010, Facebook® has more than 400 million users with the average user spending 55 minutes per day on Facebook®. The site claims that it now has 500 million users who have returned in the last 30 days (source: Facebook® Press Room, August 22, 2010). Seventy percent of Facebook® users are outside of the United States. Founded by Mark Zuckerberg with Dustin Moskovitz, Chris Hughes and Eduardo Saverin, Facebook® was launched from their Harvard University dorm room in February 2004. Facebook® now has more than 1,400 employees.

Twitter™, according to Website-Monitoring.com in April 2010, has 106 million users. At the time of the report, there were 55 million tweets, short messages comprising 140 characters or less, being sent every day – or 640 tweets per second. It's interesting to note that 41 percent of Twitter™ users have not tweeted since they opened an account. Launched in 2006, Twitter™ manages this voluminous success with only 175 employees.

Time Management Tips for Using Social Media

Social media, like e-mail, can become pretty addictive. You get involved it in, and before you know it, you have spent several hours "getting nothing important done." As with all things electronic (TV, phone, Internet, texting, social media), you must put some parameters around it in order to safeguard your time.

Here's what I do: I think about social media like taking a daily vitamin. I have a specific time in which I take it, and I check in with it at least once a day. I don't take more than I need, and I don't sit there for hours studying the bottle. Continuing with this metaphor, I try to get most of my nutrients the old-fashioned way: by eating well and living a healthy lifestyle. In networking terms, that means spending quality time with people, face to face. Social media should be used to supplement and reinforce your in-person efforts, not replace them. So use your social media responsibly, and don't completely substitute quality of contact for efficiency of texting, tweeting and the like.

How Can You Expand Your Network Using Social Media?

The first place to start is by inviting the people you already know to join you on the social media site of your choosing. Search to see if they are already there, send them an invitation and "follow" them or "friend" them (depending upon the vernacular of your selected social media site). Check out who they know and with whom they are connected. Invite those people to join you. If you see someone you don't yet know but who looks interesting to you, request that your friend introduce you through the electronic functionality of the social media site.

When reaching out to connect with them online, do your best to personalize the invitation. Mass standard communication is out; custom personalization is in. You need to make sure that you are not being generic in your communication. While social media can help you connect in the digital age, you still need to make an effort to personalize it.

If you are using LinkedIn®, be sure to create a complete online profile, listing every school you have attended, every place you have worked and every community group with which you are involved. This will tell the technology smarts behind the system to send you suggested contacts. This is a great way to reconnect with people you may have lost touch with or forgotten about. It's easy to renew connections of the past through these social media sites. It's the modern memory aid.

If you are of the mind to expand your network strategically and make specific new connections, you can mine your friends' contact lists. That is, once you are linked in with them at the first level, you can look at their contacts, which will show you your shared contacts (the people you are both connected to) and the other connections. You may find someone you know just as I did seconds ago while perusing LinkedIn®. If you know that person's e-mail address or you have worked together in the past, you can send that individual an invitation to connect with you using this vehicle. A few of these per week, and your online network will grow rapidly.

Now that You Have These Connections, What Do You Do with Them?

It's not enough just to amass a giant contact list (the numbers game); you have to activate the lines of communication. Casual acquaintances are nice, but meaningful relationships are more powerful. To achieve this online, you must do a couple of things on an ongoing basis.

1. Let your contacts know that you are still alive by posting a meaningful update at least once per week. By meaningful, I mean that you share with them what you are working on, what's coming up in your world, what new things you have discovered. We all hate the annoying trivial updates such as "I'm taking a shower" or "I just ate a tuna fish sandwich." Instead, look at your week past or present and share something noteworthy. It could be an accomplishment, a helpful resource or a combination of the two, such as "I just finished facilitating a one-day workshop on building your personal leadership brand. Check out this helpful resource on the topic" (include the link).

2. Share with your contacts your latest affiliations and achievements. You can do this by adding something to your profile, which will be shared automatically with your contact list. You might just get a few "congratulations" back, which is an opportunity to catch up in conversation online or offline.

3. Engage others in conversation. Ask for their opinions. For example: "My company is trying to put guidelines around social media usage for employees. Does anyone have any resources or suggestions?"

4. Comment on their posts. Scroll through their updates, and if one catches your eye, comment on it. This tells your contacts that you are paying attention and that you care about them. This touch point counts toward building a stronger relationship for them.

5. Recommend them. One of the easiest and most helpful things you can do for someone in your online community is to sing that person's praises and post your written recommendation online. Of course, only do this if you know the person well and can attest to the quality of his or her work. Your positive comments will add great PR mileage and could help that individual land a new job or attract new business. And it didn't cost you a dime, only a few minutes to express your appreciation and respect for him or her.

How Can You Maintain Your Relationships Using Social Media?

One of the biggest drawbacks of social media is inactivity. People notice this. You may have an account, but if you don't respond for months, it becomes very obvious and could alienate people in your community. It's a little like launching a Web site for your business and never once updating it. Nice online brochure, but not very engaging. Google will frown upon you, as will your visitors.

Regular usage is important, so you need to figure out how to include this in your daily or weekly routine. For some of you, this may require overcoming your fear of the technology monster and forcing yourself to learn a few new tricks. It will be good for you to keep your skills up and know how these new communication channels work. Don't allow yourself to become a dinosaur by making excuses like: "I don't have time to waste with that social media stuff," or "I don't like the computer that much," or "I don't want my private information out there for strangers to probe." This fear-based reluctance will only hold you back. Remember that when you were very young, you learned to stand and walk all by yourself. If you could do that as an infant, you can certainly learn how to use social media to your advantage. We are learning machines!

Keeping Up with the Youth

Here's a little insight into the Millennial Generation's use of social media from expert Dan Coates, who is president of Ypulse, a leading authority on tween, teen, college and young adult insights for marketing. The following comes from his article "Being Social" in MediaPost's on-line newsletter Engage:GenY on September 10, 2010:

> If you dig a little deeper, you'll quickly find that technology is simply a means to an end and that the end that Gen Y desires above all others is to connect ... to belong ... to be social.

> There are many reasons why this generation desires this outcome. Looking to those that preceded them, Gen Y made a conscious decision to be different from X'ers who, given their rebellious and independent nature, put individualism above all else.

> One motivation that is consistent across generations is how youth seek to establish their identity and to proclaim their existence. Here I am.

Status updates not only send a pulse out to the social network that surrounds you, they reaffirm your existence, no matter how fleeting the experience or the statement may be.

As you attempt to connect with Gen Y, make sure that you realize that technology is merely the means to an end and that the real motivator for Gen Y is being social.

The Importance of Managing Your Online Persona

For those who are younger, you must understand that even though social media is social, it is also serious. What you post on your social media sites today will impact the professional reputation that you are building for tomorrow. When I am working with professionals under 30, I often have to remind them of the critical importance of managing their online personas with care. Everything matters, and if you think that future employers aren't going to check out your Facebook® or MySpace® account as part of their hiring due diligence, think again. The photos, the comments, even your "nickname" or e-mail account name speak volumes about you. And these records are permanent. Don't be naïve enough to think that these images and correspondence won't be noticed by people whose decision-making powers will affect your future. When in doubt, don't post it. Everything matters online. It's part of how you communicate your professional image and express your personal leadership brand.

Staying Relevant

For those who are older, it can be frightening to think that the younger generations have grown up in a whole different world. They have no memory or experience with typewriters. They don't learn typing skills; they have keyboarding skills. They are less likely to have traditional telephone lines but will conduct their lives online with their mobile communication devices. In many ways, they can move, think, process and adapt much faster than older folks. They don't fear technology; they hunger for the next great app.

So how do you keep up with them? You can't just write it off as a passing phase or condemn it; you must get on board, or else you risk becoming irrelevant. These young professionals will be your future customers, your future bosses, your future caretakers. You must seek to understand, appreciate and communicate with them *their way.*

What's the solution? Work with them. Hire them to help you get with the new program. Have your daughters or sons show you how to work the social media sites. Let them be your teachers, your guides into the new way of doing things. By teaming with them, you will not only get your skills and online profiles up to date, but you also will be building a powerful new bridge with our future leaders. They too are important to add to your professional network.

"It might come in handy if we want to expand."
-Mark Zuckerberg, founder and CEO of Facebook®

15. WHO IS THE BETTER DRIVER?

How Men and Women Network Differently

"This car doesn't go very fast," was my casual complaint to my husband some years ago when I was driving a red convertible Miata. Those were the days, before kids and before I realized that skin cancer can result from too much top-down driving. I had the most incredible commute to my job at Southcorp Wines of Australia where I served as marketing manager of the hugely successful Lindemans® brand. The office was in Monterey, California, which meant I got to drive along the absolutely gorgeous coastline of Highway 101 – in a red convertible, no less. The awakening came when Byron, my husband, got behind the wheel of the Miata. I had no idea that little car could go so fast. I was gripping every handle that I could find inside the passenger cabin, just to protect myself. With a blood-drained white face and wide-eyed stare, I looked at him, and he said, "This thing will go fast; you just need to know how to drive it."

I'm not sure what the national statistics on speeding and driving records are for men and women in the United States, but in my household, there is a notable difference in driving styles and speed. The same can be said for our different approaches to building relationships.

Do Men and Women Network Differently?

Of course men and women network differently. We think differently, we communicate differently and we relate differently. Even our brains work differently, according to developmental molecular biologist Dr. John Medina, who wrote the book *Brain Rules: 12 Principles for Surviving and Thriving at Work, Home and School.* Scientists have discovered differences between men's and women's

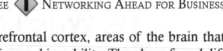

brains in the front and prefrontal cortex, areas of the brain that control much of the decision-making ability. They have found differences in the limbic system, which controls our emotional life and mediates some types of learning. And last, they have uncovered prominent differences in the amygdala, which impacts emotions and our ability to remember them.

Conversation versus Commotion:
Different Ways to Cement a Relationship

Dr. Medina goes on to cite the work of behaviorist and author Deborah Tannen, who studied gender differences in verbal capability among other things. In terms of cementing relationships, Ms. Tannen points out the following clinical observation:

> When girl best friends communicate with each other, they lean in, maintain eye contact, and do a lot of talking. They use their sophisticated verbal talents to cement relationships. Boys never do this. They rarely face each other directly, preferring either parallel or oblique angles. They make little eye contact, their gaze always casting about the room. Instead, commotion seems to the central currency of a little boy's social economy. Doing things physically together is the glue that holds their relationship intact.
>
> Source: *Brain Rules: 12 Principles for Surviving and Thriving at Work, Home and at School* by John Medina, copyright 2008, page 253.

Perhaps this doesn't surprise you. But think about it in terms of professional networking. Men tend to golf while women meet for coffee and conversation. I know that this is a huge generalization and ignores individual differences in style and preferences, but I think it sheds light on some of the fundamental differences in how certain men and women network differently. The good news is that neither one is right or wrong, neither one is better or worse. They just are two different approaches. They both can work.

Does This Stuff Work Better for Women?

Occasionally during my workshops on networking skill development, a man will ask me if my networking methods and techniques are more effective with women. This question has stopped me a few times and given me reason to pause and consider if my methodology is an outgrowth of my own personal preferences. Of course it is. But I have balanced that viewpoint by working with a male counterpart, my publisher and friend Eitan Battat. Our approaches to networking are different in many ways, but our passion and belief in the importance of building relationships to build business is the same.

Spending Quality Time with People of Influence

It has been my observation that women tend to build relationships through conversation, while men tend to build relationships through activity. Perhaps that's one of the reasons that golf remains one of the most compelling "venues" for men to network and build business relationships.

There is power in the game of golf, notably the opportunity to spend quality time with people of influence. It is the quintessential business networking activity, at least for the baby boomer generation. The jury is out on how the Millennial Generation will network. Can you golf and instant message at the same time?

Men have been leveraging the golfing "venue" for networking and relationship-building forever, it seems. Women are catching on to this opportunity. More and more women are starting to take lessons and are getting more comfortable playing golf and conducting business on the golf course. I suppose it's a new spin on equal opportunity – equal play for equal day's work.

Perhaps this doesn't surprise you. But think about it in terms of professional networking. Men tend to golf while women meet for coffee and conversation. I know that this is a huge generalization and ignores individual differences in style and preferences, but I think it sheds light on some of the fundamental differences in how certain men and women network differently. The good news is that neither one is right or wrong, neither one is better or worse. They just are two different approaches. They both can work.

Does This Stuff Work Better for Women?

Occasionally during my workshops on networking skill development, a man will ask me if my networking methods and techniques are more effective with women. This question has stopped me a few times and given me reason to pause and consider if my methodology is an outgrowth of my own personal preferences. Of course it is. But I have balanced that viewpoint by working with a male counterpart, my publisher and friend Eitan Battat. Our approaches to networking are different in many ways, but our passion and belief in the importance of building relationships to build business is the same.

Spending Quality Time with People of Influence

It has been my observation that women tend to build relationships through conversation, while men tend to build relationships through activity. Perhaps that's one of the reasons that golf remains one of the most compelling "venues" for men to network and build business relationships.

There is power in the game of golf, notably the opportunity to spend quality time with people of influence. It is the quintessential business networking activity, at least for the baby boomer generation. The jury is out on how the Millennial Generation will network. Can you golf and instant message at the same time?

Men have been leveraging the golfing "venue" for networking and relationship-building forever, it seems. Women are catching on to this opportunity. More and more women are starting to take lessons and are getting more comfortable playing golf and conducting business on the golf course. I suppose it's a new spin on equal opportunity – equal play for equal day's work.

> *"A strange game. Those that want something playing with*
> *those that have something."*
> -Cardinal Hugh Danaher, a character in John Gregory Dunne's
> *True Confessions*, speaking about golf and power (Dutton 1977)

Time Crunch

However, for many professional women, the idea of taking four hours out of the workday to spend leisure time with other business people is simply out of the question, even if their male colleagues do it as a regular course of business. Are women too responsible or too shortsighted to see what we are missing? Perhaps women need to look at this situation through a different lens. We might, therefore, consider the idea that business doesn't always have to be conducted in an office or traditional "place of business." Building and sustaining your professional relationships through sport and other enjoyable activities just might create the networking magic you need to accelerate your career and business growth.

What if You Don't Like Playing Golf?

Well, there's always food; you can network over lunch, dinner and/or morning coffee. You could go for a walk together and get some fresh air, but try not to get too winded as that looks bad for business health. Doing things together is an excellent way to enhance the relationship, as long as you are focused on the relationship as much as you are on the activity. Remember that your sportsmanship and conduct in that activity will say a lot about your character and professionalism in other contexts such as business. Don't get carried away in the winning/losing aspect of the activity. It's being together that matters in networking.

Let's Get Together for a Manicure

What other venues are available to you to conduct networking and relationship development? How about meeting for a manicure and conversation? Could you actually rationalize that in your own business mind? How about the guys?

I have a client who works for a CPA firm. She had attempted once to get a client entertainment expense preapproved by her (male) partners for an outing to a day spa with her best client. The partners balked at the idea and declined her request. One hour later, they were headed for the golf course to conduct business with their best client.

What's the Difference?

Manicure with clients versus a round of golf with clients? Time spent in any leisure activity creates an opportunity to discuss business in a more open, relaxed environment. The venue and activity may be different, but the goal is the same: strengthening the business relationship.

Whatever Floats Your Boat

My networking friend Jane shared her thoughts on the question of golf versus manicure. She said it was a matter of appreciation and motivation: "Whatever floats your boat. If they like it, do it together." In my opinion, Jane is a master connector and relationship-builder extraordinaire. Through the years, she has spent time with clients and networking contacts in all sorts of venues and activities, including the salon, the golf course, the restaurant and going for walks.

Have More Fun in Your Networking

Do men and women network differently? Thank goodness we do. We have much to learn from each other if we open our minds and appreciate our differences. Your professional network should include both men and women and people from all walks of life. Consider it a balanced portfolio. Make it a priority to build and sustain these mutually beneficial relationships with all sorts of people. Take time to find out what they enjoy doing. Ask, "What kinds of hobbies or activities do you enjoy doing?" Find out what energizes them. If you have common interests, consider the possibility of spending time together in this activity. Why not have a little fun along the way of building your professional network?

"The same things make women successful that make men successful. The main thing is desire."
-Myelle Bell, president of BellSouth International, quoted in Fortune, August 31, 1987

16. Speed Bumps

How to Network Around the Barriers

Not everyone moves at the same speed. Some people will get frustrated with you if you go too slowly, while others will get annoyed if you move too fast. When you are on "their turf," sometimes people will put up invisible speed bumps to deliberately slow you down. Rather than just plowing through these relationship barriers and potentially damaging yourself, let's explore some finessed ways in which you can cooperate with the barriers and still get what you want out of the professional networking process.

Befriending the Gatekeeper

Many of the influential people you will want to connect with will have a small army of gatekeepers surrounding them, protecting them, coordinating their every move. Many people develop a dislike for these gatekeepers, mostly because they can't seem to get through them or around them to get to the decision-maker. I think this attitude is at the very root of the problem. If you've ever been an administrative assistant or known one, you are aware that for the most part, people treat administrative assistants like the low man on the totem pole. They don't often get the respect or recognition that they deserve as human beings. Many clumsy networkers and sales professionals view these administrators as faceless, valueless voices. This is a big mistake. Why? Because these administrators have tremendous influence and knowledge of the very person with whom you are trying to connect. Finesse move number one is to take the time to get to know the administrative assistant. Know his or her name, and find out and remember what matters to them. Program that person's telephone number on your cell phone and add the individual to your professional network. Ask how you can help. Treat the administrator as a valuable person, and take the time to build a relationship with her or him, and your gatekeeper will likely give you an Easy Pass to the decision-maker. But you must earn that pass through respect and common courtesy.

Not Enough Time

Every working professional faces one major foe – the time demon. We never have enough of it, and there are many demands on it. It feels like the clock and calendar run us versus the other way around. And while we might want to spend more time with things like networking and with people and learning, the reality is there's just not enough time in the day.

If you run into time as a speed bump, don't take it personally and don't fight it. It will win every time. You must learn to outsmart time. "Be lazy like a fox" is one of the chapter headings on the new book called *Womenomics* by Katty Kay and Claire Shipman. The idea is that you must learn to work smarter, not harder or longer. The authors suggest that we put limits on our schedules and announce your "think time." They suggest that you even broadcast a rule that unless it's urgent, you'll be answering e-mails and phone calls in the mornings and late evenings. The authors also recommend to "mind your meetings" and reduce the amount of time wasted in unproductive meetings. If the meeting is not necessary or your presence is not essential (and I mean critical to the decision-making process), then graciously decline the meeting and ask to be informed of the outcome. We must learn to say "No," or if it feels better, "No, thank you."

Now, if you are on the other end of the "No, thank you" time demon management strategies, there are a few things you can do to support this effort:

1. Leave short, succinct voice mail messages with your contact information and a compelling reason to call you back. No more long-winded, cut off messages. Don't waste their time, and don't kill your opportunity.

2. Learn to get to the point quickly and put the good stuff upfront. Know ahead of time what you want to ask, and be ready with options. Learn to be comfortable thinking on your feet (and on the phone).

3. Meet on the move. Offer to drive the person or go with him or her to meetings or an event. This time in the car together can be like gold for the relationship. You are doing a service for that person and having exclusive time together.

4. Offer to bring that individual lunch. Many executives and business owners are working and eating on the run, but they have to eat sometime. Offer to bring sandwiches or coffee to their office and chat over a meal or beverage together. Food is magic!

5. Schedule networking meetings in shorter time increments, and mind the clock. Rather than asking for the traditional 30 or 60-minute meeting, request 25 or 50 minutes. Give the person this extra few minutes to take care of his or her basic needs. This shows your consideration and respect for that individual's time.

6. If you can get it done on the telephone, do it. Don't demand face time if the person doesn't have time to give that. You can build rapport and relationship on the telephone quite effectively. When the time is right, you can meet in person and appreciate each other's company.

Dealing with Skepticism

Many people are suspicious of people who "want to network" with them. They fear that this is a mask for wanting to sell something or ask for a job. If you are in business for yourself, many people will treat you like a "vendor" and keep you at arm's length. They even have special off-putting voice mail messages to send us down a convoluted path of paperwork hell. Your job as a savvy networker is to put the other person at ease with you quickly. This is most likely going to happen on the telephone, so sprucing up your phone skills and confidence is important to your networking success. Learn how to mirror and match different vocal patterns. If the other person speaks quickly, you should speak quickly; if he or she speaks slowly, you must slow down too. You may find that having someone else pave the way for your first meeting or call helps to break the ice. This can be done through an e-mail introduction or even using social media. You might find it useful to let the person know that you'll be calling them to introduce yourself. Be pleasant and friendly, but don't waste his or her time. State your intention, and suggest a time and date when he or she might be available to meet with you in person. Here's a sample telephone conversation:

> Hello Margery. My name is Kathy McAfee, and we have a mutual friend Richard Smada. (Pause for recognition.) Richard has strongly recommended that we connect and do a little networking together. I thought I'd take the initiative and reach out and introduce myself to you. Do you have time to talk right now on the phone, or would you like to schedule some time next week when perhaps we could meet for coffee? I have time on Tuesday morning, if that works for your schedule.

Your first job in the networking encounter, whether by phone, e-mail or face to face, is to put the other person at ease with you. It's called rapport-building, and this is a learnable skill that will greatly enhance your networking success.

The Budget Objection

You may find yourself running up against the budget objection. "I can't afford that right now," or "We don't' have budget now; therefore there's no reason for us to meet." If this happens to you, remind the person that your intention is not to sell anything but rather to connect and see if you can help each other in any way. There are tons of ways to create value in networking that don't involve money. There is great long-term value in creating mutually beneficial relationships before you need them. Disarm the person with a surprising statement like:

> That's OK because I have nothing to sell you. I just wanted to introduce myself and have the opportunity to get to know you and for you to get to know me. I imagine that we could both help each other in some way. That's the beauty of networking. What's open on your calendar next week?

The Black Hole of Non-Response

This is perhaps the toughest rejection of all. Your e-mails don't get opened, your phone calls don't get returned, your letters go unanswered. Don't take it personally; people are just busy and can't keep up with the inundation of correspondence. They are willing to sacrifice a little civility just to survive their day. If you are not their boss, their spouse, their child, their client or their parole officer, technically they don't have to return your call. What do you do about this situation? You get creative, and you get kind. Find a way to touch base that makes the person smile and brings joy or relief to his or her day. This is where sending personalized greeting cards or small gifts that can bring life to their day. Low-cost items such as food, garden seeds, flowers cut from your garden, travel books, family photos or funny movies from your collection can make all the difference in the world. These small acts of kindness can be huge door-openers. Be careful not to junk up their e-mail inbox with jokes, cartoons and e-cards that take more time to process and delete. This doesn't bring relief; this creates burden. If you want response, then find ways to be more engaging.

Patience is a Virtue

We all remember the lesson provided in "The Tortoise and the Hare" fable attributed to Aesop. Sometimes the more methodical and patient person wins out over the fast, arrogant and careless one. A little patience and finesse go a long way in networking and relationship-building. Slow and steady combined with caring and confident wins the race in the long run.

> *"Good friends are like shock absorbers. They help you take the lumps and bumps on the road of life."*
> -Frank Tyger, cartoonist (born 1929)

17. ONE-WAY ROADS AND EXITS

How to Gracefully End Conversations and Move On

One-way roads have always been a bit tricky for me. Some cities are full of them, and if you don't know the landscape, you can get really messed up. There are some people who just have an innate sense of which is the right way to go and when to exit. One such person is my nephew Adam. When he was only 5 years old, I took him to the Tech Museum of Innovation in San Jose, California. I had just moved back after working and living in England for three years. I had to readjust to driving on the right side of the road. After a fun-filled day, Adam and I returned to the car; I buckled him in his safety seat in the back and got myself into the driver's seat. I could see his cute little face in the rear-view mirror. As I began to exit the parking area, I was momentarily confused as to which way I should turn. The road was unfamiliar to me. I decided to turn right. From the back of the car, a little voice spoke out, "You're going the wrong way." It was eerie that such a young child would know which way to turn, but he was correct. I was about to drive down the wrong direction on a one-way street. Disaster averted thanks to the GPS instincts of a 5-year-old boy.

Zero to 60: Take Your Time in Networking

Going the wrong way in networking happens all too frequently. It can happen when you are being too pushy or aggressive, forcing a relationship to advance faster than the other person is comfortable with or ready for. This doesn't work in the romantic dating world, nor does it work in professional networking. You must give the budding new relationship some breathing space. The key here is patience and appropriate levels of follow-up.

Keep Your Eyes on the Road (Not the Visor Mirror)

Another one-way road that is overused in networking is the I-message – talking too much about yourself and dominating the conversation. You can come off as arrogant and self-absorbed to other people, or perhaps even nervous. Since I grew up with the nickname "Chatty Kathy," you can imagine that I suffer from this one-way lure.

Sometimes you have to experience someone else making the mistake before you can recognize it in yourself. I call this the buffet-moment. Here's one such time in my networking experience:

I attended a women's networking event as a guest of a former client of mine. I am still friendly with many of the women from that firm. The featured activity was "speed networking" – a cross between speed dating and networking. In this setup, we sat in round tables of eight women. We each had two minutes to introduce ourselves; the bell would ring when the time was up, and then the next person would have the floor. We went through three table rounds of this exercise. It was excellent practice and a good way to meet more of the women in the room.

When I moved to the third table, one woman – let's call her Faith –took charge immediately. She changed the rules and told us that we had to share something about our personal life. The vocal power and body language that she exhibited in her opening presentation sent a clear signal that she was bossy by nature. Rather than leading by example, she instructed the woman to her left to begin immediately. She opted to go last (nice leadership move, Faith). When it came around to her turn to speak, I was shocked to see that she broke her own rules. She bragged (and I do mean bragged) about her many professional accomplishments. She spoke nothing of her personal life until the very end, when she boasted that she was married to a military officer who was a gourmet cook. Once again the tone of her voice and gestures stripped away any humility in her delivery.

While she spoke, I noticed she started nearly every sentence with the word "I."

- I do...
- I choose only to work with...
- I am married to...
- I am certified in...
- I am expert at...
- I drive...
- I work for...
- I am...
- I...

Too Much I!

Now the I-message is a powerful interpersonal communication tool. It allows you to take ownership of your feelings and experiences and to express yourself without casting blame or triggering other people. But when you use too much I-messaging in the context of networking, you project the image of being too self-absorbed and too focused on self. You lose out on the opportunity to create relevance and to relate with the people with whom you are networking.

I drove home from the event reminding myself to keep my eyes on the road and to keep my own I-messages in check. After all, the purpose of networking is relationship-building, not the glorification of I.

Pay Attention to Other Drivers

One way to avoid the problem of too much I-message is to learn to listen and ask more questions. Make it your goal to learn something new every time you meet with people. Learn to retain that knowledge in your short-term memory. Don't allow it to escape instantly (in one ear and out the other), but make sure you retain at least some of it through active listening. I love to preface my questions with the phrase "I'm curious about ... ." If you can get the other people to open up and talk about themselves, then you are going to be credited for being a great conversationalist.

You might want to practice what my friend Marge calls "the art of being in service of others." Be "others-centric," rather than "me-centric,"and make it your first priority to get to know the other person. This takes all the pressure off you to give your elevator pitch or your 30-second commercial. Marge suggests starting with open-ended questions such as, "Tell me about yourself." Notice how different that feels from the more direct work-related question that everyone expects to hear and hates: "What do you do for a living?" Marge's question allows people to share more about themselves than just their job, which may not be their passion. It's hard not to like someone who expresses genuine interest in learning more about you.

Which Exit to Take?

Perhaps the most stressful moment in networking is the awkwardness of not knowing how to gracefully leave a conversation. You don't want to get stuck with the same person all evening. Quality is important, but in networking, you need to pay attention to the quantity of connections as well. Sometimes you find yourself clinging to certain people out of fear of meeting new people. Other times, people cling to you. If neither party is skilled or confident in graceful exits, it could turn a nice connection into a long, dull and boring one. In networking, you must learn how to exit and move on to new roads.

There is an art to the graceful, confident and natural exit, where people can end their conversation and move on to meet other people without feeling weird about it. This you need to practice and get good at. You'll need to do it to be successful in networking. You must learn not only to say "hello," but also to say "goodbye, see you later."

Here are a few tips on how to get good at the exit.

- **Be direct:** "I think it's time for both of us to move on and mingle with the other guests. Shall we?"

- **Signal the close:** "I've enjoyed our conversation. May I follow up with you after the meeting?"

- **Take a break:** "If you don't mind, I'm going to get a drink." Or, "If you'll excuse me, the ladies room is calling."

- **Be a connector:** "Oh, there's Sally Fraser. May I introduce you to her?"

- **Be humble:** "I have dominated much of your time. You need to meet more people. Thanks for speaking with me."

- **Add more people to the conversation:** When you sense other people around you, use open body language and hand gestures to invite them into your conversation. When the time is right, leave these two people and move on to another cluster. "I think you two have a lot in common. I'll leave you so you can get to know each other better."

- **Excuse yourself:** "If you don't mind, I need to go check on something. I've enjoyed our conversation."

- **Exchange business cards:** "Before I depart, can we exchange business cards?"

- **Get the other person's permission:** "I see an old friend that I'd like to reconnect with. Do you mind if I part your company?"

- **Wish the other person well:** "I'll take my leave now. I hope you have a great evening and meet many interesting people."

- **Let the other person go:** "There are many people here tonight you'll want to meet. It's been a pleasure connecting with you. Enjoy your evening."

Of course, body language and vocal inflection will be an important part of making any of these responses work. Be careful not to start with "scanning eyes" – looking around the room to see to whom else you can talk. This sends a very negative message to the person with whom you are currently networking. While you are with that individual, give him or her your full attention. When you decide it's time to move on, do so with respect and dignity.

"There's a trick to the Graceful Exit. I begins with the vision to recognize when a job, a life stage, a relationship is over – and to let go. It means leaving what's over without denying its value."
-Ellen Goodman, American journalist, Pulitzer Prize
winner for Distinguished Commentary (1980)

18. Odometer versus Speedometer

Gauging the Pace of Your Networking Relationships

Think about the dashboard on your vehicle. How frequently do you look at the speedometer – the meter that tells you how fast you are going at any given moment? It's the point of contention for many drivers who are pulled over by police officers for exceeding the speed limit. We couldn't have been driving that fast!

Driving fast is exciting. You feel as if you are getting somewhere. It makes you feel as if you are the master of your own destiny.

Now think about your odometer. How often do you look at this gauge? How do you feel when you see the miles on your car piling up? Does it make you feel old or worn? You know, closer to that oil change date? Do you feel with every mile driven, as if the resale value of your car is declining?

In networking, these two gauges are also very important: How fast you can build new relationships and how long will those relationships last? Going fast versus going the distance: Which is more important for you in terms of building mutually beneficial relationships?

Find Your Cruise Control

Once you master a few of the networking skills and employ some of the networking strategies that you will discover in this book, you will be able to put your networking efforts on cruise control. That means you'll be able to drive at a reasonable speed – one that is safe and that you consciously choose – and you'll get better gas mileage, enabling you to drive longer on the same amount of gas. Cruise control will keep you out of traffic court, will reduce the stress on your body while driving and will help to optimize the performance of your vehicle. What's not to like about cruise control?

What Does Cruise Control Look Like When You Network?

- You are not rushed to develop the relationship. You take a long-term view of it and build it through time. The value of the connection is not a destination but rather a journey.

- You are less stressed about the relationship. You discontinue the jerky stop-start motions that you may have done earlier. The relationship-building process becomes more fluid and natural for you.

- The process of follow-up is more automatic. You don't really have to think about it; you just let it roll. When you think of this person, you reach out in kindness. You check in more regularly, because you care about the relationship. You are less focused on the immediacy of the networking exchange and more focused on seeing a bigger, longer-term picture.

The Dangers of Going Too Fast

Here's a story about how I learned the benefits of using cruise control in my networking strategy. In this particular case, I needed to slow down and not force the relationship in order to ensure its longevity.

I considered my former colleague Mary Lou to be a good friend. We had worked together for two years; she was my right hand on the job. I served as a professional reference for her on several occasions. I admired her many skills and loved to brag about her to potential employers. She also helped me in a very significant way. She hired me as a consultant to help one of her new colleagues prepare for a very important internal presentation. This emergency presentation coaching session became my first success story and laid the foundation for my high engagement presentation coaching program called "The Motivated Presenter." (Download *Clean Sheet Thinking,* a trademarked presentation planning tool that's free from MotivatedPresenter.com.)

In my enthusiasm and thirst for business growth, I pushed too hard with Mary Lou. I began to look to our relationship for more business development. Mary Lou was not prepared for that and she reacted toward me. I backed off and gave it a rest to let the irritation heal and repair. I checked in with her every few months to see how she was doing. She occasionally responded, and I began to wonder if we were really that close.

Then Mary Lou got laid off, and I was one of the people she called upon for help. She confessed to me that she was a reluctant networker and had realized that this was a big weakness for her. She was gainfully re-employed within six months of losing her last position – not bad given what was going on in the labor market at the time of this writing. She told me that the biggest lesson that she had learned in this process is that she must always keep up her networking, when she is working and when she is not. I am optimistic that this lesson will stick with her, and her attitude and behavior about networking has fundamentally and forever changed. Time will tell.

But I also learned a valuable lesson from this experience. You can't expect everyone to give as much as you do or even give what you desperately want and need them to give to you.

The value of the relationship is much bigger than any referral, job assignment or transaction that may come your way as a result of knowing this person. My behavior and expectations toward Mary Lou had put our relationship in jeopardy. I was going too fast and too hard. I needed to back off on the gas pedal and adjust to a more comfortable speed for her.

Going the Distance with Your Relationships

The cool thing about using the cruise control feature when you network is that you can adjust it as you go. You can accelerate and decelerate as you need. If the new networking relationship needs a little more urgency or is moving at a faster pace, you can easily speed it up. If on the other hand, you sense that your new networking friend is crazy busy and time-starved, you might want to back off a bit, slow it down and let the relationship take more time to develop. Your goal is to become a long-distance driver and networker. You are going the distance with all the relationships you build. You want a high reading on your networking odometer!

"The tortoise, winner of the race, Stood proudly in the winner's place. The moral of this tale, I'll say, Is 'Slow and steady wins the day.'"
-*The Tortoise and the Hare*, a fable attributed to Aesop

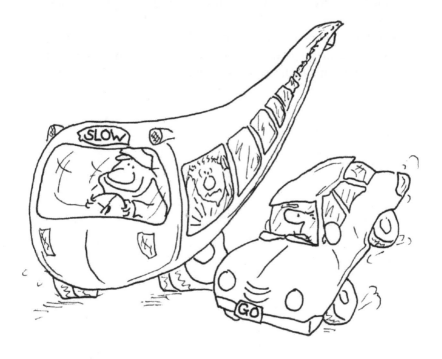

CHECKLIST #3

You are almost there! You've completed Part III of your networking journey. Part IV will give you resources and inspiration to make you a motivated networker for life. Complete these actions and you will be ready for Part IV.

☐   I understand how to leverage networking as part of my business development strategy. I am confident in discussing business opportunities with people in my professional network.

☐   I regularly ask other people that I know to help me by facilitating "warm introductions" to new people that I wish to add to my network.

☐   I have a strong presence on the major social media sites. I have completed my profile and uploaded a professional-looking photograph so people can easily recognize me. I actively invite people to connect and interact with me using on-line channels.

☐   I have mastered the art of conversation and know that listening and asking questions are important in the communication and relationship-building process. I keep my ego and "I messages" in check and focus more of my energy on getting to know other people.

☐   I can confidently work a room, starting and ending conversations with ease. I can mingle without feeling awkward and regularly practice the "be the host" networking technique.

PART IV

ARRIVING AT YOUR DESTINATION
TAKING YOUR NETWORKING TO THE NEXT LEVEL

19. PARK NEXT TO THE LAMBORGHINI

Networking with People with Money and Influence

Do you consider yourself rich? Could you stand to be richer? Of course, you could. Now we can and should define wealth in broader terms, not just financially. There's the wealth of good health and vitality. That you cannot buy. There's the wealth of strong, loving and healthy relationships. There are riches that come from possessing a good attitude and having imagination and creativity at your disposal. There's the power of positive motivation and determination – that's worth a fortune. And then, yes, there's money, assets and access to it.

No matter what your current circumstance in life, no matter how many miles your odometer shows, you too have the opportunity to stretch out of your comfort zone and start networking with people of greater influence and resource than you have. The reality is you must, if you want to go anywhere and do anything significant with your life and career.

When I lived and worked in Europe I was always surprised when I would run up against "classism" – the classic battle of "haves" and "have nots." It's a classic cultural divide that has lasted for eons. Yet some people manage to overcome it and leapfrog from their current station in life to new, higher levels.

In this age of information and technology, where innovation and motivation can triumph against any obstacle, real or imagined, we all have the potential for greatness. But it takes a great deal of gumption to go and get it. And you can achieve that through your professional networking.

Consider a young teenager named Jackson (not his real name). At the time of this writing, he was a senior at a magnet school in Connecticut. I met Jackson while I was teaching a networking class to the school's film class, as part of my community service. I was actually doing a favor for a networking friend and fellow Soroptimist Sharon and her incredible husband. They are involved with the school as members of the Business Community Advisory Board, which creates internships, mentoring and other resources for the economically underprivileged, but highly motivated and brilliant students at the school.

Jackson was one of the first students to greet me. He was personable, confident and handsome, I recall, and gave me a firm, professional handshake and looked me in the eyes while he introduced himself. This quality and action I always admire – at any age. Jackson quickly expressed his personal brand when he threw me an odd-ball question during Q&A. He asked me if I knew a good recipe for guacamole. This was precisely the kind of question that the teacher had warned the kids not to ask their guest speaker. But I fell for it and started listing off ingredients to make the perfect dip. I saw Jackson again at the annual Business Partnership Breakfast, where he was serving as the master of ceremonies. Once again, he was charismatic, confident, bold and prepared. When the school principal spoke, he mentioned that Jackson would always have a place in his heart because he was the first student to welcome him to the new school and to shake his hand. Jackson figured out at the age of 15 that parking next to the Lamborghini is smart. Why not the rest of us adults?

Step Up Your Game

If you are serious about creating strong career and business success for yourself, then you must step out of your comfort zone and start networking with people of greater influence than you. You will need people with more resources (including higher-level connections and relationships) to get you introduced and exposed to higher-level opportunities. Waiting in line with everyone else may be the polite thing to do, but you'll be waiting for a long time and you may not get it. You need greater access.

You need to associate with people who can connect you to the right places and leaders. It's time to accelerate and supercharge your networking efforts.

Here are a few things you can do to get yourself into position for people of influence to advocate for you:

1. **Do your research.** Know who's who in your targeted community. Find out more details about them, including their background, their families, their hobbies and interests, the things that they like and don't like. Who is currently connected to them? Where do they hang out?

2. **Be where they congregate.** Invest in purchasing tickets to charity events, conferences, golf and social clubs they are known to frequent. Make an investment in your own career by purchasing access to the places where they gather. Perhaps you have to start out as a golf caddy, but at least you'll have close personal time with them and know their strengths and weaknesses. This is one of the ways in which Keith Ferrazzi, Mr. Relationship and author of *Never Eat Alone,* got his big break.

3. **Ask for what you need.** Practice making your pitch before the real thing. Make it crisp and compelling. Make it short. Give the person a powerful reason to help you. Be persistent. Don't take no for an answer. You may irritate the individual, but he or she will admire your tenacity. This is the trait of a leader.

Join the Board

People of money and influence often have a philanthropic spirit. They feel compelled to give back. They also enjoy the political and social power and visibility that comes with being on nonprofit boards of directors and committees. That's a great place to meet them. They are more open to new ideas and new people. They are out of their traditional work environment and are less likely to block your entrance.

By signing on as a board member or committee member, you may also benefit from the richness of mission-driven work. What might have started as a personal networking motivation will soon morph into something more powerful – giving back and serving the greater good. This is when you will be at your very best and will become naturally attractive to people of power and influence.

You must let your intentions be known and ask to be considered to nonprofit board positions. And you must be willing to carve out significant time and energy to devote to and fulfill this new community leadership role. Your "performance" in this capacity will be a demonstration of your worth to the people with whom you are trying to connect. Once you earn their trust, they will open their Rolodex™ to other people of influence and resource to you.

Finally, you must be patient – very patient. People of money and influence are used to people sucking up to them and seeking them out. They are in demand, not because they are wonderful people, but because they can provide for others. It is natural that they are cautious and suspicious. Your approach to them must be authentic, professional and positive. They will quickly sniff out the fakes, phonies and fearful.

Respectfully Equal

It is important that you present yourself as a confident person who is capable of providing good value. You too have resources and the ability and willingness to help others, similar to them. Your body language and use of voice must convey strength. Eye contact is critically important, as is your handshake, for these two nonverbal actions will send an instant signal to the powerful person with whom you want to connect. Your bank balance may be currently less than theirs, but your self-esteem and belief in your intrinsic self-worth is on par or better. You are not afraid to hear "no" because you know that "no" is a power word, and you respect it highly. If someone is unwilling or unable to help you,

you have the courage and conviction to ask who else he or she knows who might be in a position to assist you.

Ultimately, you both put your pants on the same way – one leg at a time. You both have the same organs – heart, lungs, kidney, liver, etc. You are both equally susceptible to disease, illness and heartache. You both have the opportunity for greatness in what you personally achieve and whom else you help achieve it. You both have something to gain by helping each other in networking.

> *"Position yourself as a center of influence – the one who knows the movers and shakers. People will respond to that, and you'll soon become what you project."*
> -Bob Burg, author of *The I Go-Giver*

20. DRIVERS WANTED

Be a Connector of People

You often hear companies proclaiming, "People are our most important assets." Yet company policies and practices are often directly in conflict with this core value. The same holds true for people and networking. We say that people are important to us, but then we take them for granted, ignore them for long periods of time and reach out to them only when we need them. This is not walking the talk.

The graduate level of networking is when you become a master connector – a person of influence who connects other people together. You actively share your connections with others, and encourage them to meet and get to know each other. You are the talent development director and a relationship management specialist. You see the potential magic that is possible when the right people come together. And you are the kind of person who makes that happen frequently.

When you do this, you will not only have developed a new core competency (i.e., people skills), but you will also have a valuable new asset on your balance sheet – more fans.

This section is focused on how you can become a connector by adopting simple practices and a shift in mindset.

Seeing the Connections

When you network with people, you need to use your peripheral vision. You need to be actively thinking about who this person should be meeting after you. Who else do you know who would benefit from meeting this person, or who else do you know whom this person could help? You need to be scanning for similarities – shared values, shared interests, shared experiences. This is the basis of a good networking connection – people with common ground.

As a master connector, you will find that you start to do this naturally. You just think this way. It's an unconscious competence that you possess. Other people you network with are not yet at this level. Your initiative to help introduce them to others is in essence modeling excellence. You understand at a deep level that putting people and ideas together is a powerful thing to do. You see beyond yourself. You are future-oriented. You are willing to help other people, even if they are reluctant or scared to meet other people.

Facilitating New Introductions

One way you can help people in your network is to facilitate introductions for them. What do I mean by that? You help people relax and get to know each other when they are meeting for the first time. You take the burden of starting the conversation between them. You get things going.

Here are a few ways in which you can easily do this:

Live and In Person: You can do this at a party or meeting, when you are face to face, by intentionally setting out to introduce your friend to other people. You help to position that person well by stating a few things that the individual might have a hard time saying about himself or herself. Act as a publicity agent and give testimony about what you value about your friend.

Three-Way: If you host a three-way lunch, three-way coffee or three-way dinner, you are bringing two people together with you to help oversee it. This requires a little more investment of your time and energy (and sometimes your money), but you will benefit as well. This approach ensures that the connection actually happens. It goes better when you bring these two people together and help to facilitate their conversation. You strengthen your relationship with both of them, and get the joy of seeing a little networking magic happen. Try it out.

Telephone: You can facilitate introductions over the telephone. You can call both parties and let them know you'd like to introduce them to each other. Get their verbal agreement, and alert them that you'll be sending their contact details via e-mail. Or if you have three-way conference calling, you could do it live on the spot. This can work magic, but it also can put people on the spot when they are not ready to talk.

E-Mail: You can facilitate introductions through e-mail by writing to both parties and encouraging them to connect. I like to provide basic contact details such as e-mail and telephone numbers to make connecting convenient. I also write a few sentences about why I think they would make a good connection. I wish them "happy networking" and invite them to let me know how it goes. Please note: The probability of people acting on an e-mail introduction is lower than if you do it in person or over the telephone. It's easier to ignore e-mails, you might be catching the person at a very busy time, or be the 110th e-mail in the inbox. It's easy for e-mail to get lost.

Social Media: You can also introduce people via LinkedIn® and other social media sites. LinkedIn® has a function called "Forward this Profile to a Connection," where you can share the profile of someone you know and trust to someone else in your LinkedIn® contacts who would be a good match. You can also request new connections using the "Get Introduced through a Connection" functionality. Both of these approaches require that you write a personal introduction. I have had success using both but do find that it is still fairly passive, and most people are slow to respond.

Jerry, Meet Kendra; Kendra, Meet Jerry.

I was helping my friend Kendra with her job search. I remembered a very cool connection I met at a technology convention. I searched for his card and picked up the phone to dial Jerry to see if he'd like to speak with Kendra. I actually got him on the phone, but I could tell that my approach was putting him on the spot. He said to me awkwardly, "I can't talk right now, I have a newborn baby in my arms." This turned out to be very important information. I was able to congratulate him, both on the phone and by sending him a card. While I wasn't able to connect Kendra immediately on that day, I secured permission from Jerry to contact him later to set up time to speak with her.

Now Kendra was a reluctant networker and she didn't follow up as I had hoped she would. I decided that I would hold her hand a bit more and take a drive down to Jerry's facility to introduce them personally. He had invited us both down for a tour and discussion.

It was a great day and a terrific opportunity to catch up with Jerry and to help him with a visionary entrepreneurial project – one that I believed in strongly as well. The three-way visit made it easier for Kendra to meet and network with a "stranger" whom now she knows. She was able to ascertain that Jerry's company would not be a good fit for her, which was good information to know. However, she made a new connection. And I reconnected with Jerry and strengthened that relationship. I'm not sure where it will go or what it will lead to, but I felt good about helping Jerry, Kendra and myself through this facilitated introduction.

Be the Host

One of the easiest ways to get comfortable in networking and to improve your connecting skills is to practice the strategy called "Be the Host." It works like this: Whenever you go to a meeting, conference or gathering of people, pretend that it is your party and you are the host. As the host, it is your job to make sure that your guests are welcomed, introduced around and are having a good time. It would be rude of you to spend all of your time with just one guest, so it is expected that you will mingle among all your guests. If it were your party, you would take a more active role in introducing people to each other. You are facilitating introductions.

When you act the host, you have a higher energy level and a more welcoming demeanor. You are less nervous or worried about yourself. You are unlikely to be the "wall flower," shy and reserved. And you also are doing great service to the official host – by helping to start conversations and ensuring the guests are enjoying themselves. The gathering is more likely to be successful because of your efforts. (You might just find that you are invited to more events!)

Get a Seat at the Table

When you become a connector of people and expand your sphere of influence, you will have an easier time getting a seat at the table, that is, being invited to participate in higher-level meetings, organizing committees and other places and spaces where people of influence gather. By showcasing your people skills and natural ability to bring people together, others will see you as a leader. You will have secured yourself a seat at the table for more interesting conversations.

The best personal example of this is my work and involvement with the YWCA. The YWCA is the oldest, largest multicultural, multigenerational women's organization in the world. I met the wonderful people of the YWCA through a networking connection facilitated through my career coach at an outplacement agency. Rhonda introduced me to her friend Deb, who, at the time, was serving as the chairwoman of the board of directors of the YWCA, in addition to running her own consultancy firm. Deb graciously invited Rhonda and me to be her table guests at the YWCA's "In the Company of Women" luncheon, a fabulous fund-raising luncheon that is packed with 1,500 women and men from the community who are motivated to help fulfill the YWCA's mission of empowering women and eliminating racism. It was a grand day, and, of course, I followed up to thank Deb and Rhonda for the opportunity.

Deb then facilitated an introduction with Deborah, the interim executive director of the YWCA (now the CEO of the organization). I did a little pro-bono work for them. It then turned into a short marketing engagement – my second client after I had launched my new business. This was a wonderful way to get to know what the organization stood for and to understand the tremendous value that their programs and services provide to our community. I also met fabulous people on their board of directors, their staff and their supporters. Between their mission and their leaders, it was hard not to get the YWCA fever. I become a passionate advocate.

Fast forward five years later: I am on the board of directors of the YWCA of the Hartford Region. I have met very influential and interesting people – all who share my passion for helping to improve the lives of women and girls (who, in turn, help improve the lives of families, communities and the world). This step up in exposure, learning and connections has been phenomenal. And it all started with a facilitated introduction by my career coach Rhonda to Deb, a woman who was a stranger to me at the time. These two women gave me a seat at the table. It can happen to you too.

Meeting Important People

You meet important people when you become an important person. And you never quite know when that is going to happen. But I can tell you *how* it will happen.

You become an important person when you help other people achieve their goals. You become important to them when your relationship goes from casual acquaintance to strategic friend. You have gained mutual trust through time and they are now comfortable opening up their Rolodex™ to you. They advocate for you. They introduce you to people whom you otherwise might not know or might have a hard time meeting by yourself.

You become an important person when you realize that you too are important. This starts with the basic assumption that you are valuable, regardless of your current circumstances. It's called self-esteem. You have to have it. It is the bone marrow of your self-confidence. If you don't have self-esteem or an intrinsic belief in your self-worth, then your body language will show weakness. Your voice will have a quality about it that suggests it's not worth spending time with you. Your inner critic may take over and influence your choice of words when you make that all important call. You have to be confident in how you approach other important people. So here it is: You are an important person. I bequeath you. I knight you. I give you the crown. Wear it well.

You become an important person when you make more of others' time. Important people are in demand. Because of their position, authority, influence, power, resources and connections, many people want a piece of their time and attention (and sometimes their money). Everyone wants time from important people, and that's something that they have little to spare. Therefore, you shouldn't waste their time; rather, you should be strategically thoughtful about how you could help them so that they get more of what they want. At the end of the day, important people are people, too. They have needs. They have feelings. They have challenges. They have dreams and goals, too. You can become important by fulfilling these needs. You can do this.

You become an important person when you have new ideas and take calculated risks to challenge a dysfunctional status quo. Important people are inundated with yes-people – people who agree with them all day long just to stay on their good side. Leaders eventually get bored with the yes-people and seek out people who will challenge their thinking. The people closest to them have the most risk and have the hardest time doing this. But you, as a new connection, have nothing to lose and everything to gain. Be bold. Be helpful and stretch this leader's thinking. You may find yourself becoming valuable to an important person whom you want to add to your professional network.

Teaching Others

When you become a connector of people, you will take on the role of teacher and mentor. You will be guiding others in the art of networking and helping to acquire this valuable professional skill. Your example will help them to adopt a more positive attitude towards meeting people and building relationships through networking. You will be giving back to others in ways that will surprise you. All the while, you and your business will continue to grow as a result of your skilled networking You are leading and prospering by example. You have arrived.

"I must admit that I personally measure success in terms of the contributions an individual makes to her or his fellow human beings."
-Margaret Mead, in *Redbook* (1978)

21. Plot Your Course

Design Your Own Networking Roadmap

There are many different ways of traveling. Some people, like my husband, Byron, have a spontaneous "Go North" attitude. Others, like me, like to map out every detail, be highly organized and know exactly what comes next. Perhaps this is the "perceiver" and the "judger" aspect of the Myers-Briggs® personality types shining through. Whatever your style, you can benefit from developing an action plan around your networking goals. Why? Because for most people, networking is not part of their normal routine, and, as such, it becomes a low priority, if not a completely ignored strategy. This entire book has been about heightening your awareness and increasing your motivation toward making networking a key strategy now and for the rest of your life.

What Are Your Networking Goals?

What do you want to achieve with your networking relationships? Why and how can they serve you? What other goals are they connected to? By setting goals, and making them SMART goals (more on that later), you are more likely to achieve success. Once you taste a little success in networking, your confidence builds, and you begin to do it more often. Success begets success. You build momentum in your networking. Before you know it, you can become a master connector.

Building SMART Networking Goals

The SMART goal system means that you set goals that are: specific, measurable, attainable, realistic and timely. This is different from setting BHAG goals: big, hairy, audacious goals. Both types of goals are important and have their place. However, in order to start the momentum-building process in your networking, I recommend that you start a bit more grounded in your approach and leave the lofty, stratospheric goals for another time.

Can you determine which of the following networking goal statements qualify as a SMART goal?

1. To network with top executives who can help me grow my business.

2. To connect with all of the Fortune 500 company leaders who are located in my state.

3. To meet and network with five of the top 20 Fortune 500 company executives who reside in my state by December 31 or sooner.

Now, all three of these goal statements are positive and on target; however, the third one is the most "doable." This is because it was written with the SMART goals in mind. Notice the dates and numbers and reasonableness of the goal. It is still a stretch goal, but is much more attainable than the idea of meeting all of the leaders. You can see the natural next step of research to identify the list of the Fortune 500 companies with offices in the state and the executives in charge. Getting to this level of specificity will greatly increase the probability of you achieving this important goal.

Now that You Have Your Goals, What Do You Do Next?

Congratulations! You have written down your networking goals and have put them through the SMART goal test. You have refined them so that they are specific, measurable, achievable, realistic and timely. Your next step is to build a strategy to achieve it. Strategy is all about the how. Networking and relationship-building are in themselves a strategy, but we don't want to stop there. We want to drill down and get very specific on the how. This is where the action plan comes into play:

- **Goal:** To meet and network with five of the top 20 Fortune 500 company executives who reside in my state by December 31 or sooner.

- **Strategy:** Leverage my professional network to get introduced to these executives;

- **Action plan:**

   1. **Research:** Conduct research to learn more about these companies and executives. Short-list the names to the top 10 who appear to be the best fit for me and what I have to offer. Timing: Complete research by *[specific date]*.

   2. **Who knows whom?** Use LinkedIn® to find out who in my network is connected to anyone at these companies or who personally know these executives. Timing: Complete this step by *[specific date]*.

   3. **Share:** Talk about my specific goal with my Top 50 most important networking contacts. Let them know what I am doing and why, and ask them if they know anyone who could help me achieve this. Follow up on any and all leads or connections they provide to me. Timing: Ongoing activity.

   4. **Connect with influencers:** Make connections and network with people who know these executives well and could introduce me in the future. Get to know these influencers, and build trust with them, for they too will add value to my network. Demonstrate my value to these influencers by offering to help them achieve their networking goals. Timing: as opportunities present themselves.

   5. **Be patient:** Be persistent. Be flexible. Visualize goal achievement. Timing: This will be an ongoing, daily activity.

6. **Build rapport:** When I meet these executives, I will focus first on building rapid rapport with them. I will let them know succinctly who I am and what my specialty is. I will listen intently for their needs, pain points and hot buttons. Find out their birthdays (research online or just ask), and take note of what is important to them personally and professionally. I will plant seeds and ask for their permission to stay in touch over time. Timing: immediate, in the moment.

7. **Follow-up:** After I have met these executives, I will have a game plan for how I can stay visible and valuable to them. Showcase my uniqueness and motivation by sending personalized cards every three months or so. Be relevant and ready for when their timing is right. Timing: first follow-up within three days of meeting; thereafter, touch base quarterly.

What if You Are Just Getting Started?

Perhaps you are not planning on taking over the world and want a less intense action plan. No worries. We can handle that. In fact, there are a number of basic action steps you can take to prepare yourself to become more connected and more influential in time.

Here is a suggested three-month action plan that anybody can do to get the networking process rolling. All it takes is a little discipline, some time and persistent motivation.

Month 1: Desired outcomes: Identify your active network and create your online presence.

a. Week No. 1: Make a list of everyone you know. Use the My World Exercise spreadsheet to group people by affiliation and connection to your life. (Download a free template at NetworkingAhead.com.) In this step, you just need their names. Don't waste your time searching for their contact information. That will come later.

b. Week No. 2: Give thought to which of these connections is most important to you. With whom do you have the closest relationships? Who can help you the most? Who are the most connected and influential people you know? Whom do you care about the most? Are those feelings mutual? Would they return your phone calls promptly? Select from your master list the people who fit this description. This is the beginning of your Top 50 contact list.

c. Week No. 3: Set yourself up on LinkedIn®, Facebook® or Twitter™. Include a professional photograph (if you don't have one, get one.). Fill in your profile with sufficient background information on the jobs you've held, schools and affiliations. If you need examples of how to craft your profile, check out other people's public profiles or check out a book from the library on the subject. Your profile is an expression of your personal brand; give it some reflection. Remember, you can always modify it in the future. This is the beauty of online.

d. Week No. 4: Research different contact management systems. Select one that is right for you. Begin to input the contact details into your system from your My World™ Exercise spreadsheet. Invite these same people to link in with you on LinkedIn®. If you don't have their full updated contact information, ask for it, so that you can input it into your contact management system.

Month 2: Desired outcomes: Start reconnecting with people you know, make new connections and grow your professional network by at least five people (or one new person a week). Attend a networking meeting this month. Get more organized with a contact management system.

a. Week No. 1: Reach out to one person in your network every day via telephone, e-mail or social media. Complete five touch points this first week. Schedule a date to meet one person for coffee or lunch within the next two weeks.

b. Week No. 2: Dive deeper into LinkedIn® and other social media sites. Review the connections of the people to whom you are linked. Find someone on their list of contacts whom you'd like to meet, and use the system to request an introduction. When you find people you already know, but have not yet linked up to, send them a personal invitation to link in. Do this once daily and accumulate five or more new contacts.

c. Week No. 3: Attend a local networking meeting, either as a member or as a guest of a member. Groups to consider include your local chamber of commerce, BNI® group, community service groups (Soroptimist, Rotary, Civitan). If your company hosts onsite meetings for specialty groups, such as Toastmasters, women's alliance or other special interest groups, consider attending and introducing yourself. Bring plenty of business cards, and go with the intention of making three to five new connections that you will follow up.

d. Week No. 4: Follow up with the leads and connections you made last week. Add these new people to your contact management system. If you need administrative help to get this done and it really isn't your forte, hire an assistant to set it up for you and update it. It is critical that you develop an organized and efficient system that works for you. Do this early, and it will make your networking life a whole lot easier and more fun.

Month 3: Desired outcomes: Start investing more time and energy into your Top 50 contacts and strengthening those relationships. Continue to add new connections to your professional network. Attend another networking meeting this month. Get serious about follow-up. Demonstrate consistency with daily visits to your preferred social networking media site.

a. Week No. 1: Touch base with 10 people from your Top 50 contact list, and strive to add value to their day. Ask them how you can help them, and tell them whom you are looking to meet specifically. Think of whom you could connect your Top 50 people with, and help to facilitate the introductions. Update my "networking activity" on LinkedIn® by listing one key thing you are working on right now. Add, do or change something with your social media account.

b. Week No. 2: Continue with your Top 50 outreach. Check in daily to social media. Schedule networking coffee or lunch with a new contact within the next two weeks. Attend a networking meeting and make three to five new connections. Add these folks to your contact management system.

c. Week No. 3: Top 50 outreach. Check in daily to social media. Follow up on the connections that you made last week. Send them a greeting card and invite them to join your online network through LinkedIn® or Facebook®. Offer to introduce them to other people in your network who you think would make a good connection. Facilitate that introduction.

d. Week No. 4: Top 50 outreach. Check in daily to social media. Find interesting articles, blogs, books or other content that you think would be valuable to selected people in your network, read them yourself and then send some to the selected people in your network (via snail mail, social media or e-mail). Ask for their feedback on the content. Engage them in a dialogue, and encourage them to share this information with others in their network who would benefit from it.

When you bring together focus, motivation and a solid action plan, any goal is achievable. I encourage you to plot your own course for networking success. With every day and every week that goes by and you are "doing it," you will find it becomes easier, more natural and infinitely more successful for you. In no time at all, you will build your networking confidence and competence. The professional network that you build will become one of your strongest and most powerful assets.

> *"If you don't know where you are going,*
> *any road will take you there."*
> -Lewis Carroll, *Alice in Wonderland*

22. Fuel Extenders

Resources to Get Greater Mileage from Your Networking

There are products on the market today that claim they can extend your fuel mileage, reduce your emissions and renew the life of your engine – all without having to buy a new hybrid car. The claims sound great, but few people buy. We live in a skeptical world, and we are creatures of habit. Some might call us downright lazy.

Your professional network, much like your car, is a machine with a limited warranty. You take for granted that it will keep running for you, and most of us just like to "gas and go." When it breaks down, we get angry and blame the manufacturer. But somewhere deep down, we know that the buck stops with us. We own the car, after all, and it's up to us to take care of it. It is of our making if we run it into the ground and neglect its maintenance.

The same can be said for your professional network. You don't have to be a mechanic or an expert to look after what you have and to ensure it runs smoothly for you for a very long time. There are resources that are readily available to you right now to help you maintain your professional network and get greater mileage and a better ride from it. You will need to take action and make some investment in order to benefit from these great networking fuel extenders. Here are some to consider adding to your mix:

Fuel-Extending Tools

1. Contact Management System is a must-have for any serious professional who wants to build and maintain a robust professional network of people who can help you achieve your goals. Don't try to reinvent the wheel when the market has provided many excellent tires for you to choose from. Being organized and having contact

information available at your fingertips wherever you go is more than a convenience; it is essential to your networking productivity. A contact management system is like the infrastructure of your networking enterprise. Things must be organized in order to run well.

2. The SendOutCards® system not only offers a strong contact management system but also gives you a tool that allows you act on your promptings and reach out in kindness to people in your network. SendOutCards® is a technology-backed greeting card and gifting company that allows you to send handwritten cards and postcards instantly to your clients, networking contacts, friends and family anywhere in the world through a functioning postal delivery system. It combines the best of new technology and service with the old-fashioned joy of receiving something personal in the mailbox (not just another e-mail message or e-card). Here's how it works: Select a card from one of their 15,000 card designs, type your handwritten message, add photos if you like or scan your business card as an image, select the mailing address from your contact management system and press "send card." The company then prints it, puts it in an envelope, puts a real stamp on it and mails it for you. All for a fraction of the cost and time of running to the retail store and the post office to send this kind of personal message. If you'd like to try out the system, you can go to my site at MotivatingCards.com.

3. Social media is a great networking accelerator, enabling us to merge our personal and professional networks and connect with people all around the world with ease and effectiveness. You owe it to yourself to get up to speed on these fast-advancing technologies that are geared to help us reach out and stay in touch with people we know and people we want to get to know. These systems are ideal for introverted personality types who are less eager to meet people face to face, but are still motivated to keep in

contact. Like any great fuel extender, you must be careful not to overdo it. Too much time spent on social media can quickly become counterproductive to both your results and your relationships. Put parameters and limits on your use of social media. It is a great addition to the mix of how you network, but don't let it dominate your life.

4. Thin Threads® Custom Books is an awesome tool for sending inspiration to the people in your network. This technology application, which was created by my beloved publishers Eitan and Stacey Battat of Kiwi Publishing, is one more step toward empowerment of the individual to create content and publish his or her works. What they have done is collect and professionally edit real-life stories of life-changing moments from people like you and me. They then have put those individual stories online for us to select. You pick the cover design, you select the stories that you want included in the custom book, you write a personalized inscription on the inside front cover and you provide the mailing address of the person(s) who will receive your beautiful gift. They print it, they put it in an envelope, they mail it for you to the person(s) of your choosing. This innovative and personalized tool can enhance your networking relationships in ways that traditional communication cannot. For less than the cost of lunch, you can send a custom book packed with inspiration and thoughtfulness that will stand out and last for months. To try out this system, go to CustomizeMyBook.com and order your first custom book for someone in your network.

Fuel-Extending Knowledge

1. Books on networking allow you to study and put into practice skills, insights and techniques that will last you a lifetime. Networking and relationship-building is ageless and timeless – there is always something new to learn and a new approach to try. Some of my favorite networking

books include: Keith Ferrazzi's *Never Eat Alone* and *Who's Got Your Back;* Susan Roane's *How to Work a Room;* Diane Darling's *The Networking Survival Guide;* and Steve Harper's *The Ripple Effect.* Your local library or bookstore is filled with tons of great resources. You may find as I did that reading just one chapter or one section may give you the boost you need to take your professional networking activity forward.

2. Networking Tips are available to you at the Web site NetworkingAhead.com. Opt-in for the *free networking tip of the week* and make an effort to apply the technique or idea immediately. Practice and experimentation is key to building your networking savvy and success. You can also join in on our networking conversation on Facebook®. Become a fan of the book at NetworkingAhead.com/ Facebook.

3. Articles and blogs are perhaps a quicker way to get new ideas and go-power to extend your networking momentum. You can also easily share them with people in your network by forwarding the link or posting it on your social media site. Check out the blog at MotivatedNetworker.com.

4. Conferences and events that include networking as part of their programming are also excellent places to advance your knowledge of networking. The great part also is that you are in an environment where you can immediately start applying what you have learned. Everyone attending the conference has come to make new connections and is potentially more open to trying out some new networking approaches. Conferences and conventions give you plenty of opportunities to practice your networking skills in a concentrated, low-risk environment.

Fuel-Extending People

1. Positive, motivating people who inspire you and push you to be a better person are great enhancements to your network. Don't allow yourself to be bogged down with negative, pessimistic or toxic people. You can subtly disengage from these people by reducing your investment of energy and time in them. You don't have to have a difficult confrontation with them; you just need to migrate away from them. E-networking connections, like friendships, are optional and at-will relationships.

2. Your Top 50 contacts are great fuel extenders to your networking success. These are the people you've decided to invest more of your time with because these relationships will bring the greatest value to your life. These people are folks you have strong relationships with and who care about your success. They will return your phone calls promptly and will go out of their way to help you in any way they can (and you will do the same for them). These people should fuel you with positive energy, encouragement, feedback, resources and motivation. If they don't, perhaps they don't belong on your Top 50. Replace them with people who do.

3. Your local chamber of commerce is a fantastic fuel extender for your networking and business success. The more involved you get with your chamber, the more value you receive. It's a direct correlation. Quality input yields quality output. Mine all of the resources that they offer their members. Attend their regular events. Build strong relationships with the staff and the other members. Bring in new members to make the organization richer and more interesting for you and others.

4. Networking groups and organizations that fit well with your personality and pursuits make great fuel extenders. Sometimes you have to try out a few to find the right fit.

You may also find value in serving as a substitute for others who belong to a BNI® group, for example. With schedule realities, you are going to have to choose which networking groups you want to engage with on an ongoing basis. We can't belong everywhere and do everything well. Time and sometimes money are limited resources, so choices need to be made. Give yourself the time to personally experience and evaluate different networking groups until you find the one(s) that work best for you.

5. Civic groups and community service organizations are outstanding places to extend your networking power. You come together with people who share a similar passion and do mission-driven work together. You are pooling your talents, time and treasury to advocate for and provide support to people, projects and problems that need fixing. Along the way, you get to know your fellow civic members in deeper, richer ways, not just by what they do for a living. These connections will surprise you with their present and future value. I recommend professional women and business women check out becoming a Soroptimist, which means "best for women." Learn more about this volunteer service organization, its mission and good works at Soroptimist.org.

Fuel-Extending Motivation

1. Music, exercise and healthy living are guaranteed to help you put more positive energy into your networking and professional relationships. Worn out, uninspired and unhealthy people don't have much to offer others. Your efforts to take great care of yourself mean you will be able to bring more to the table for yourself and for others. You can't take a pill for this; you need to get up and move your body.

2. Goal-setting and action plans are great fuel extenders for both your professional development and your network. By

putting measurable goals into place and creating an action plan, you can make visible progress in your professional development. What gets measured gets done. Imagine where you will be a year from now, if you start today.

3. Carrot-and-stick incentives can be very effective in helping you get out of your comfort zone and make a serious upgrade in the caliber of your networking efforts and outcomes. Figure out what motivates you and create incentives (positive or negative) that work to move you to action. If you need help with the taskmaster role, engage someone who knows you well to be your accountability buddy. Make your incentives tangible, visible and immediate to make them more effective at driving daily behavioral change and action.

"It is inevitable when one has a great need of something one finds it. What you need you attract like a lover."
-Gertrude Stein, 1957

23. THE ROAD LESS TAKEN

The Networking Journey to a More Rewarding Life

As we come to the end of this book, I am inspired to call upon the profound works of two amazing thought-leaders: the poet Robert Frost and M. Scott Peck, psychiatrist and best-selling author.

Robert Frost's poem *The Road Not Taken*, published in 1916, speaks to the tough choices people have to make when traveling the road of life. Inevitably, you have to leave some possibilities unexplored as you make choices and move forward in your career and life. Wouldn't it be great if we could do it all, experience it all and have it all? The exciting news is that networking expands your possibilities as you amass and carry with you a growing number of mutually beneficial relationships to support you on your life's journey. It is limited only by the time, energy and commitment that you put into it.

Dr. Peck's profound book *The Road Less Traveled* was first published in 1978 but didn't become a best-seller until 1984, some six years later after he hit the lecture circuit and personally sought reviews in key publications (there's a testament to persistence and personal conviction). If you haven't read this amazing personal manifesto for living in a while, I suggest you pick it up or read it again. His insights on the value of discipline and its connection to our emotional, spiritual and psychological health can also be applied to the health of our professional and business lives. He outlines in depth why the ability to delay gratification is good for us, a character trait that has significantly waned with the daily advancements in technology. His commentary on accepting responsibility for oneself and one's own actions continues to be highly relevant and needed in our world. This is perhaps the essential starting point for individual empowerment and real change. Playing the blame game and living with excuses will never get you very far or make you truly happy.

These philosophies of living are precisely the qualities that will make you more successful in your business and professional life – discipline, patience, personal responsibility, authenticity and positive intention. Developing these philosophies into daily working habits will enrich your relationships in any sphere of your life.

Part of Larger Purpose

In the middle of writing this final chapter of this book, I was called away to speak at the Total Woman Conference, to give a workshop on networking and to help facilitate connections among the hundreds of women attending this event sponsored by Princess Bola Adelani, president/founder of Royal Proclamations. If you are wondering if she is a real princess, you'll have to go to her Web site and read the last paragraph on her bio on the "About" section of the Web site: RoyalProclamations.com.

This divinely inspired conference opened my eyes once again to the magic of networking. I connected with women from all walks of life, from different cultures and different faiths, but we all had once thing in common: a burning desire to do something special with our lives. We were all there seeking answers to some of our burning questions, some of which could be found in the simple act of meeting new people and beginning new relationships.

In addition to my role as a workshop speaker and facilitator, I also had a trade exhibition booth. Yes, I wanted to sell stuff. I had invested significant time and money to prepare my booth from staffing, to materials and display, to the free prize draw and devices to engage the guests to come and talk to us at our booth. But at the end of the day, it wasn't about the value of immediate transaction or trade show sales. I sensed something much larger. I could see the future power in these budding new relationships.

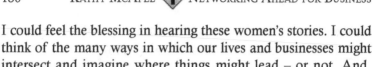

I could feel the blessing in hearing these women's stories. I could think of the many ways in which our lives and businesses might intersect and imagine where things might lead – or not. And, of course, I knew that following up on these new connections and nurturing these new relationships would be paramount to realizing the future benefit for each of us.

The Road to Mutually Beneficial Relationships

Throughout this book, we have discussed that networking is essentially the art of building and sustaining mutually beneficial relationships *before you need them.* It is a win-win-win game. It takes energy, motivation and discipline to play the networking game well. And it can be tons of fun in the process. If you commit to studying the art of networking and applying its techniques, tools and attitudes into your daily life, you will quickly find yourself on an exciting new journey that you won't ever want to end. The destination stop-offs will be rewarding and memorable, and you will want to go back for more and more. You can never outgrow networking, never be too young or too old to do it, use it and enjoy it. It is an ageless, timeless professional skill, if not an essential life skill. It will help you get where you want to go.

Networking Is a Strategy for Life

Some of you reading this book purchased it to solve a real and immediate problem, such as unemployment, the desire to land a better job, launching a new business or securing your next client. Your motivation to apply the networking skills that you've learned in this book is clear and compelling. I encourage you to go for it. Try it out. Put those ideas into practice now, and measure your success. Leverage networking to achieve your next goal.

I also want to encourage you to go beyond that immediate short-term goal. I invite you to continue on the journey of building long-term relationships for the rest of your life; to permanently alter your personal definition of networking from an event or an activity that you have to do at certain times in your work life to a core strategy for creating a successful career, business and life for yourself and others you care about. I invite you to join me and become a motivated networker.

Enjoy the ride.

America's Marketing Motivator

> *"I took the one less traveled by, and that*
> *has made all the difference."*
> -Excerpt from "The Road Not Taken" by Robert Frost

FINAL CHECKLIST #4

Congratulations! You've arrived. You've completed all four parts of this book. You have acquired the networking skills and confidence to practice the following business beliefs and behaviors:

☐   I am a connector of people and actively practice putting people and ideas together, even if it doesn't benefit me directly. I see beyond myself.

☐   I consider myself to be a student of networking, constantly seeking out new information and new experiences in order to enhance my mastery of the art of networking. I teach others what I have learned.

☐   I am strategic and thoughtful in my approach to networking. I have a road map and action plan to guide me to my desired destination in business and in life.

☐   I actively seek to increase my sphere of influence by networking with people of greater power, influence and resources than I currently have. I know that I too can bring value to these new networking relationships. Together we can create greater value and more opportunities for ourselves and others in the world.

☐   I understand that networking is not an event or an activity, but a strategy for life. It has become an integral part of how I conduct business, how I manage my career and how I guide my life.

INDEX

W

Y

Z

Numbers

ABOUT THE AUTHOR

Kathy McAfee is America's Marketing Motivator, a professional speaker, leadership coach and communications trainer, certified in Neuro Linguistic Programming at the master practitioner level. A seasoned marketing professional, Kathy has over 25 years of corporate and international business experience with the likes of Levi Strauss & Co., Maybelline Cosmetics and Southcorp Wines of Australia, as well as five years as a successful solo-preneur.

As president of Kmc Brand Innovation LLC, she serves as executive presentation coach to motivated business leaders and ambitious entrepreneurs to help them become the recognized leaders in their field by mastering the art of high-engagement presentations and more effective networking. Kathy is a card sending enthusiast and her independent distributorship of SendOutCards® can be found at MotivatingCards.com.

A graduate of Stanford University and a black belt in the martial art of Tae Kwon Do, Kathy currently lives with her husband and two boys in Simsbury, Connecticut.

Learn more about Kathy's business, visit MarketingMotivator.net

Become a Facebook® fan at NetworkingAhead.com/Facebook

GET FREE
NETWORKING TIPS

from Kathy McAfee
America's Marketing Motivator

Scan this QR Code with your smartphone
to receive free weekly networking tips.

http://networkingahead.com/networking-tips/sign-up/

Kathy@MarketingMotivator.net
www.NetworkingAhead.com
Like us on Facebook